15485

# THE
# COMMUNICATION
## OF THE
# CHRISTIAN FAITH

# THE
# COMMUNICATION
## OF THE
# CHRISTIAN FAITH

*by* HENDRIK KRAEMER

15455

*Philadelphia*
THE WESTMINSTER PRESS

# PREFACE

THIS SMALL BOOK CONTAINS THE FIVE LECTURES THAT WERE given by me as the 1955 Laidlaw Lectures at Knox College, Toronto. Illness prevented me from delivering them in September, 1955, as originally planned, and so they were delivered from January 30 until February 3, 1956. I gladly avail myself of the opportunity to express my deep-felt thanks to Knox College, which invited me, for the honor they bestowed on me, and for the warm hospitality so many people showed to Mrs. Kraemer and myself.

I should like to ask my readers to be patient with the compact style of this presentation. The compass of five lectures forced me often to be far too brief on many points, and to leave out others.

HENDRIK KRAEMER

# Contents

# 1 *Communication in Biblical Perspective*

EVERYWHERE IN THE WORLD, IN DIFFERENT DEGREES AND tones, the Christian Church finds itself on the way to re-discovering, re-evaluating, and restating its marching orders. Necessarily implied in this conspicuous trend is a re-thinking of the Church's true being, calling, and destiny, and of its relation to the world and all its spheres of life. The ecumenical movement is undoubtedly the greatest stimulating factor in this trend, strengthening it where it was already developing and fostering it where it was still dormant. To what end all this will lead is, of course, un-predictable, but with joyful gratitude one dares to say that the Holy Spirit is breathing in many places. It is, for in-stance, impressive to observe how the old Church of Abys-sinia, for long centuries isolated and self-contained, is be-ginning to enter the great ecumenical fellowship of the Churches. The beginning is, indeed, modest enough, but the possibilities and promises hidden in such a small event are great, because this Church is now being drawn into the " trek " on which the Churches at a different pace have embarked.

Our thinking, still so largely determined by the fact that our Churches are *established* institutions, with *established* rights, privileges, and disadvantages, is beginning to real-

9

ize that the Church is by its nature a body on pilgrimage, "reaching forth unto those things which are before." It would mean a spiritual catastrophe if, for instance, the World Council of Churches in fact became mainly the organized effort for reunion and mobilization of the separated Churches, thereby forgetting its true inspiration, that is to say, being an Abrahamitic adventure of faith toward a still unknown country, which God will show to us.

One of the most important effects of this trek set in motion by the attempt to rediscover the marching orders of the Church is the new awakening of evangelistic responsibility to the world in many Churches. But here bewilderment begins. At the very moment a Church commences to turn away from the introversion in which it is steeped by its acceptance of being primarily an established institution, and looks at its real field, the world, a new realism awakens. Innumerable questions immediately assail such a Church, such questions as: What am I? To what purpose am I? Am I fulfilling this purpose? Where and how do I live? In a ghetto, or in living contact with the world? Does the world listen when I speak to it, and if not, why not? Am I really proclaiming the gospel, or am I not? Why has such a wall of separation risen between the world and what I must stand for? Do I know the world in which people live, or do I not? Why am I evidently regarded as a residue of a world that belongs irrevocably to the past? How can I find a way to speak again with relevancy and authority, transmitting "the words of eternal life" entrusted to me?

Amidst the welter of such questions, engendered by a newly awakened apostolic consciousness, communication has become a problem with which the Churches everywhere are wrestling. Apparently one could express it as well in a different way and inquire after the best and most appropriate methods of evangelism. But that is not right. In that case we would have done better by giving to our discussion the title " The Problem of Evangelism." The word " communication " puts the problem in a far wider and deeper setting, wider and deeper because in the word " communication " two aspects are brought together, both of which are of vital importance. Communication is " the fundamental human fact," as Roger Mehl says in his fine booklet *La Rencontre de l'autrui* (p. 7) . The essence of our humanity lies in this fact. Mehl adds, quite rightly, that communication as the fundamental human fact has not only to do with language — often it even transcends it. This essential aspect of communication we propose to call *communication between,* and it leads to the realms of theology, of sociology, and of psychology: theology, because the core of all true evangelism is communication, transmitting the creative spark of the regenerating and converting word by witnessing to it; theology also, because there is a genuine theological problem implied in the strange fact that the fundamental human fact, communication, manifests itself more in its frustrations in human life than in its achievements, more in its failures than in its successes. Sociology and psychology are involved because the intersubjective relations of men, manifest in communication, are favorably or unfavorably influenced by sociological and psychological factors and situations necessitating a clear distinction between different levels of communication.

There is, however, another aspect of communication, which we propose to call *communication of.* For our purpose this aspect is, of course, of the utmost importance for the simple reason that whether we enter into the implications of *communication between* or of *communication of,* our main concern is the communication of the Christian

message, which, by its very nature, aims at the deepest communication, that is to say, the togetherness in the communion with Christ. Moreover, our special concern is the communication of the Christian message in a world that seems
to be separated by a deep gulf from the deepest thought,
language, and true ethos of the Church. What are the possibilities of bridgebuilding? Or is that pluriform, chameleonic phenomenon which we call " the modern world " so
utterly alienated from the range of the Christian message
that bridgebuilding is an illusion? In saying this, we do not
artificially assume a pessimistic attitude but we are thinking of a sentence in one of the preparatory Evanston reports on evangelism, where it is said that, globally speaking,
it must be conceded that the Churches have become im-
potent evangelistically.]

*Communication of* and *communication between* must,
therefore, be distinguished, yet at the same time be kept
together. Well understood, communication of the Christian message, if it achieves its divine end, that is to say,
engenders a new creature in Christ, works at the same time
in principle the right communication between, the right
intersubjectivity. It is because of this polar interrelation
between the two aspects of communication that we begin
by presenting some reflections on communication in Biblical light. Perhaps this may affect some readers as rather
remote or as evidence of the European predilection for in-
troductory Biblical statements on everything on earth and
in heaven. A psychological or phenomenological analysis
of communication seems more natural at the start of a discussion on communication than at a later stage as we shall
do. There is, to be sure, much to be said in favor of this
standpoint, especially that it is more congenial to our
modern habits of thinking and approach. It seems to bring

things more down to earth. Moreover, in itself there is
nothing against looking at the subject on the purely human
plane of psychological observation and phenomenological
penetration. There is an enormous gain in trying to look
at things as they present themselves to careful and, as far
as possible, unprejudiced scrutiny. One could even defend
the thesis that Churches and Christians in particular stand
in great need of this exercise, and I for one very often defend this thesis. Yet in this case it seems to me more appropriate to start with some observations on communication
in Biblical light, although I am fully aware that the questions and approaches directly implied in *our* cultural and
psychological analyses with regard to the problem of communication are as such not to be found ready-made in the
Bible, and are, therefore, not directly answered.

[There are no ready-made answers in the Bible to any of
the questions of the modern world. But if it is true that
communication is the fundamental human fact, the hallmark of our humanity, yet more conspicuous by its failure
than by its success in the history of human life, then it appears that in this whole matter of communication the kind
of understanding of man we have is central and basic. It is
the peculiarity of the Bible that, according to Christian
experience, it gives basic answers to such basic questions,
because its main burden is to spread before us human history as God's risky adventure with man, from creation
until consummation. ]What we hope to find there is the
*right orientation* and the *right foundation* for our problem
of communication so that we begin by understanding it
from within, that is to say, from the angle of God's intention and purpose with man. Turning first to the Bible,
the record of how God dealt and deals with mankind in
acts of revelation, while investigating this thoroughly hu-

man issue of communication, amounts to the confession that man is a mystery in himself and to himself, that he cannot be explained out of himself, but can be understood only in God, his Maker. In the Bible understanding in God means essentially understanding in the light of Jesus Christ, through whom we understand. Thus, one understands as " the new man, which after God is created in righteousness and true holiness " (Eph. 4:24). In the light of Christ we not only get the right understanding of man in his contradictory complexity and as created for community and, therefore, for communication, but we understand also the imperious character of the communication of the Christian message.

The point constantly stressed in the Bible is that God alone knows man in his inner motives and being, and that therefore the knowledge of self goes through the knowledge of God, and not the reverse. It is said of Jesus Christ that he knew what is in man (John 2:25). Psalm 139 is one of the grand documents that insist upon this fundamental starting point. " O Lord, thou hast searched me, and known me." " Search me, O God, and know my heart: try me, and know my thoughts." In the prophetic writings of the Old Testament more than once the expression recurs that God alone knows and tries the reins and the heart of man (Jer. 11:20). All these and kindred sayings are spoken out of the ambiguous situation of man, knowing and yet not knowing himself, knowing and yet not knowing each other. The fundamental vision of the Bible is that God, being the real ground of man's being, has created man for communication with him, or as the profound Roman Catholic writer Ernst Michel puts it, for dialogue with him. This theotrope character of man, to use an expression of Dostoevsky's, is the ground for their being created for communication with each other. Authentic humanity reposes therein. God has created man as his partner and ally to live in communion and communication with him and so with each other, because only in this way the heart of man is in the right place, while oriented in the right direction. This is the divine *natural* law of man's existence and destiny. But here the term " natural law " has a meaning quite different from the usual one.

The God of the Bible is a God who speaks. One of the well-known, outstanding characteristics of the Bible is the great recurrence of the expression: the word of God coming to man. The word is the symbol par excellence that stands in human intercourse for communication. The meaning of this constantly recurring speaking of God is not only that he is the Lord, who commands and thereby creates, but also that God wants personal relationship and invites to personal relationship as the fulfillment of human existence." God, who at sundry times and in divers manners spake in time past unto the fathers by the prophets, hath in these last days spoken unto us by his Son, . . . the express image of his person "(Heb. 1:1–3). In these words the dialogue, the communication of God with man, is summed up in the light of the dispensation of Christ. God's history with man is seen under the angle of a continued discourse. The true and deepest sense of this manward divine urge permeating the Biblical record of God's peculiar character finds expression in the name Immanuel, " God with us," given to Jesus Christ, the Word made flesh.

This immediate, personal relationship, or, in other words, this communication of God with man as the foundation of the true life, finds a striking expression in another aspect of the phraseology peculiar to the Bible. Combined with the expression of a deep awe of God's majesty, holiness, and greatness, in short, of the mystery and inaccessibility of God, there is on both sides, on the divine and on the human, a deep intimacy of tone and relation. " You are *my* people, I am *your* God " rings through the whole of the Old Testament. The psalms are filled with the desire for the closest relationship with " *my* " God. The close personal nature of God's communication with man, and on this basis of the communication between men, is, in the Old Testament, put under the viewpoint of man's response in *love* to God's speaking to him. This response in love is the only adequate expression of full communication, of man's whole-hearted acceptance of founding his life on the dialogue with God. Deut. 6:4, 5: " Hear, O Israel: The Lord *our* God is one Lord: and thou shalt *love* the Lord *thy* God with all *thine* heart, and with all *thy* soul, and with all *thy* might "; and Lev. 19:18: " Thou shalt love *thy* neighbor as thyself: I am the Lord." Our Lord Jesus Christ, when asked about the chief divine commandment as the basis and source of the true life, combined these two verses with intuitive sureness. Love is that state of mutual transparency, disposability, and responsiveness in which true communication comes to full fruition. This is what the Bible has to say, in essence, about communication as the fundamental fact between human beings.

In this light we must see the fact that in the Bible the concepts of the covenant, the people, the church as the " *koinōnia* " of the believers with Christ and in him with each other are so central. God wants a people whose hearts are bound together in him. Christ prays for a church in which the members are one in the Father and in him. The peculiar community of Israel has its *raison d'être* and calling in the divine covenant, in an act of divine sovereign establishment of relationship. This community of Israel is not founded in its biological, cultural, or even sacral unity. The sacral unity is rather an expression of the community established by God. In so making the people of Israel the instrument of his redemptive will and purpose in regard to the whole of mankind, it is called a "holy people." The two classical passages are Ex. 19:4–6 and Deut. 7:6–12. What has this to do with our subject? This, that according to the Biblical view one can have God, have full life, only in community. The " I " and the " thou " are both founded in God's will and life-giving power. Therefore both are responsible to God and to each other, related to him and to each other, unthinkable without communication as the law of human nature. Dietrich Bonhoeffer has elaborated this viewpoint in a very interesting way in his book *Communio sanctorum.* When our Lord is asked by his disciples to teach them that sublime act of personal relationship which is prayer, he teaches them to say: *Our* Father, give *us,* . . . lead *us* not. God is not a God of isolated religious individuals, but of a people, the people of his Kingdom in which communication will be perfect.

We repeat: this is what the Bible essentially has to say about communication as a general and fundamental human fact. As such the Bible vindicates it fully and establishes it in the divinely willed order of existence, in the nature of man as created by and to him. But this is only half of what must be said, although the most important half. The other half is that communication, which is so essential to human life and also to human nature, seldom succeeds and often fails. Is that sufficiently explained by our human finiteness? Can we overcome it by trying to understand each other? The Bible has a different answer which is quite consistent with its view of communication as the specific human quality. This answer runs on this line: If the calling and aptitude toward communication in man is rooted in his right relationship to God, his Maker, Judge, and Redeemer, then the distortion of communication, its dangerous and delicate place in actual human life, must go back to the distortion of this primal relationship. The fact that our humanhood is not normal, but abnormal, in a fallen state, that is to say, fallen out of the right communication with God, is the evil source of a corruption which becomes manifest in all relationships, in all patterns of communication. Defectiveness in communication is a sign as well as a consequence of the distortion of the divinely willed order of existence. The break of real communication in human life, which perpetually characterizes our personal, social, economic, and political relations, filling human life with anxiety, fear, and frustration, is the result of a primordial break of communication with God in whom we nevertheless live and move and have our being. In other words, the whole drama of communication with its partial successes and recurrent failures through which mankind moves in history is essentially and fundamentally a religious drama.

This fundamental fact is described in a naïve but very impressive way in Gen., ch. 3. Man, fallen out of his partnership relation with God, flees from God, and immediately all relationships are affected and in disorder. The dismal play of self-assertion, the one against the other, the maintaining of one's right by accusing the other, begins. It goes even deeper. Man immediately practices the art of self-justification by accusing God. " The woman whom thou gavest to be with me, she gave me of the tree, and I did eat." The deepest of human relationships, that between man and wife, is vitiated. Labor, which is meant as a blessing, as a partnership with God in creative activity, gets the stamp of a curse. Cain kills his brother Abel, and gives the tragic answer ringing through all the ages when God calls him to account with regard to his brother: I know not where he is. Am I my brother's keeper? In the parable of the Good Samaritan, our Lord gives the antiphon to this cry of hideous callousness by telling the lawyer: Don't ask who is my neighbor. Know that you are always the neighbor to the other. Language, the typical symbol of unity and communication amongst men, the instrument to meet each other, becomes the source of misunderstanding, disruption, and deceit. In human life it assumes the ambiguous role of communication and frustration of communication. Every human creature, all human relationships, in all spheres of life, suffer under this ambiguity and yet exploit it. The self-contradictory state in which the human urge for communication manifests itself has its roots in the self-contradictory state in which man lives with God.

With regard to the whole matter of "communication between" viewed in Biblical light, it is very essential to remind ourselves that the Bible is in the first and last place the record of God's history of salvation with man and the world. Only the *re*-creation, the *re*storing, of the right relationship with God can be the basis of the re-creation of true unfrustrated communication with each other. This is one of the deep meanings of the Church, to be the place and sphere of this re-creation of true communication, because its function is to be the true community, founded through Christ in God, the embodiment of renewed humanity.

It is quite consistent that the Bible, presenting God as the originator and establisher of true relationships between him and man, and between man and man, presents him also as the initiative taker for restoring the communication after it has been broken. "The Lord God called unto Adam, and said unto him, Where art thou? And he said,

I heard thy voice in the garden, . . . and I hid myself." In these two expressions — " Where art thou? " and " I hid myself " — the dialectic in the communication between God and man is fully contained. Translated into theological terms, this means that although man still hears the voice of God ("I heard thy voice in the garden "), he flees from him, and therefore the Bible does not describe the religious history of man as a quest for God, but as a divine seeking after man; in other words, " *Heilsgeschichte* " as God's persistent act. God wills to be with man in order that they will be with each other in him. This is " *Heilsgeschichte*." The German word " *Heil* " expresses better what is meant than the English word " salvation," which has become accentuated in the direction of rescue and redemption, which are more restricted in meaning than " *Heil*." From the point of view of etymology the word " *Heil* " is akin to Sanskrit " *sarva* " (i.e., whole) , Greek " *holos*," Latin " *solus*," which is " *totum*." Connected with these words are the Latin " *salvus*," which means " without fail," " whole " and " healthy," and " healing." The " *Heliand* " or " *Heiland*," i.e., the Saviour, is the " whole-maker." " *Heil* " presupposes that which is broken and then restored to wholeness, to full integrity. The Old Testament concept of "*shalom*," the significance of which has been so ably demonstrated by Johs. Pedersen, rests on the same background. The adequate translation is not peace, but wholeness, integrity, *Heil,* the state of complete integration of a community, its restoration into its original God-willed design. To proclaim " *Heil* " is in Hebrew " *dibber shalom*," " to speak peace." " *Shalom* " is, therefore, the sign of Messianic times. In this sense the *Heilsgeschichte* has as its purpose the remanifestation of the unbroken relationship of man with God, and of men with each other. Jesus Christ could, therefore, announce it as the Kingdom of God, a new realm of unbroken communication. God's way to work this " *Heil* " is by his entering into concrete human existence in Christ, in whom all things will be gathered in one. He is, therefore, the Saviour, the Bringer and Effecter of *Heil* and wholeness. As Barth says in his *Kirchliche Dogmatik* (III/2), in Jesus' " state of being with man," in his " being there for man," it becomes manifest that " the togetherness of man " is the natural fundament of human life.

In Jesus Christ, the decisive and only authentic Word of God comes to man. In him the image of God in which man was created becomes gloriously visible. In him all things are reconciled to God, i.e., he overcomes the broken relationship, reopening the way of communication. In him it is possible to be one in the full sense of the word, in spite of all differences and divisions which separate men and hamper or frustrate their communication. In principle, Jesus Christ is the sole ground on which full and true *communication between* can become effective. In him " the fundamental fact " can regain its proper place and significance, because in and through him there grows a body, a new community, which stands in the world with a new hope.

At this turn we have reached an important point. In Jesus Christ, who changes in principle the total human situation, because in him the new realm of faith, hope, and love as a divine gift enters the corrupt body of mankind, the two patterns of communication, that is, communication between and communication of, appear as closely connected. The communication of the Christian message, which is in fact the heralding of Jesus Christ as the reconciliator and the reintegrator of the broken pattern of human life, is, in principle, the most direct way both to uncover the hidden cause of disordered human communication and to discover the way back to its real meaning.

In the whole range of forms in which *communication between* human persons takes place, there is, of course, also a good deal of *communication of* implied: communication of ideas, doctrines, emotions, instruction, values, information, appeal, and so forth, with the whole possible gamut of partial or full response, indifference and defiance, which is evoked. Here the question rises: Is communication of the Christian message one species of the many forms of communication, of interhuman discourse, or is it a category of its own? In Biblical light, it is the last, although we should see quite clearly that to the profane eye and ear it is just one of many forms of communication only specified by its subject matter. This last opinion is in most cases strengthened by the fact that the communicators of the Christian message transmit it in a way entirely identical with those who in their communication try to convey to others the Christian message or something else as the truth of a body of doctrines or values.

Why then, in Biblical light, is the communication of the Christian message to be regarded as a category of its own?

First, because of its *peculiar character*. It is not a message about which the bearers have the right to decide whether it should be communicated or not, whether one should keep it as a precious private possession for oneself or not. It *must* be communicated because it issues from the prophetic consciousness that it is the Word of the Lord of the universe: " Hear, O heavens, and give ear, O earth: for the Lord hath spoken." It has called a community into being, the *Church,* which exists for the sake of the world, and not for its own sake. The communication of this message of divine *Heil* and healing to the world is the thing for which

the Church exists: "That thy way may be known upon
earth, thy saving health among all nations" (Ps. 67:2). It
is an unending task. Communication of the message is the
crowning category of which all activities of the Church in
evangelizing, preaching, teaching, and witnessing to all
fields of life are part. It is also a task that must constantly
be restarted. There is no part of life, nor of the world,
which is ever definitely evangelized. This incessant communication of the Christian message is what we presently
call the missionary or apostolic obligation of the Church.
What Paul says in II Cor. 5:14 and I Cor. 9:16 about himself is valid for the Church as a whole. "The love of Christ
constraineth us " — the love *of* Christ, not in the first place
the love *for* Christ. The communication of the gospel is not
a "*kauchēma,*" i.e., a cause for glorification, but an
"*anagkē,*" i.e., a divine must, laid upon the Church. When
Jesus Christ, after his resurrection, meets his disciples, he
makes them into his apostles by saying, "As my Father
hath sent me, even so send I you." The sending of his
Church into the world is the continuance and reflection of
the worldward divine urge which became manifest in Jesus
Christ even until the death on the cross.

The Christian message conveys the revelation of God, not
of an idea of God which enters into competition with other
conceptions of the divine. Revelation means that God wants
to be known, not to be known *about.* God discloses himself in his acts in concrete human history by opening his
heart and making known the "mystery" of his saving will
in order to commune with man. Dietrich Bonhoeffer beau-
tifully says that the Church is "founded in the revelation
of God's heart" (*Communio sanctorum,* p. 97). Every deviation from this Biblical realism is a deviation from the
true communication of the Christian message. Therefore,

the New Testament so frequently uses the expression " *kēryssein to euangelion.*" Our translation of " *kēryssein* " as " preach " hopelessly weakens its meaning. It is only adequately rendered by " proclaim," because it is not a transmission of doctrines or truths, but the proclamation of an all-decisive event, which in principle changes the whole situation of the world. It is the proclamation of the " *basileia tou theou,*" of the Kingdom of God, of the new world, embodied in Jesus Christ. Through the proclamation the Kingdom comes, and at the same time the proclamation is an appeal to prepare ourselves for it and accordingly change our hearts *(metanoia)*. *Because God's Kingdom has come,* the hearer ought to change his heart, not in the first place because his heart is evil, as the writer in Kittel's *Wörterbuch,* under " *kērygma,*" aptly remarks. Our Lord when " ordained " by baptism, by the descent of the Holy Spirit, and by the temptations by the devil proclaimed the gospel of the Kingdom of God, saying, " The time is fulfilled, and the kingdom of God is at hand: repent ye, and believe the gospel." We have learned to make a distinction between " *kērygma* " and " *didachē* " (= teaching), but " *didachē,*" which is not pervaded by the life breath of " *kērygma,*" is not a really authentic communication of the Christian message. In the New Testament the proclamation, the communication, always has the character of the announcement of God's acts, happened for us, and of the invitation to enter into the stream of this divine history.

The Christian message is, therefore, not communicated in the name of our experience — not because experience is not relevant, but because it is not basic. It cannot be, because it does not prove anything. Experience of God can be matched by a different experience of him. It is basic that God's acts which have established a new redemptive reality which is a challenge to the hearer are announced. It is, therefore, typical for the New Testament that the communication of the message does not in the first place appeal to the understanding of the hearers, but appeals to their faith, that is, the surrender of their hearts as the only adequate response to God's revelation of his heart. At Pentecost the crowd heard the apostles proclaim " the wonderful works of God," and not their undeniably marvelous experiences of their Master. It must be said with all emphasis possible that this does not mean a depreciation or rejection of subjectivist witness, and a recommendation of objectivist witness, in the terms of the controversy raging among theologians and in various sections of the Church until the present day concerning subjective and objective preaching. As usual, the Bible transcends such categories, which we invent in various historical situations in order to mend, although imperfectly, one-sided emphases in which we have erred in proclaiming the gospel.

In the Bible the proclamation of the gospel is always an indissoluble unity of subjectivity and objectivity, because its true nature is prophetic. The prophets of the Old Testament are at the same time the greatest objectivists and the greatest subjectivists. Their sole and entire concern is the Word of God that came to them, but their whole heart, their full experience and grasp of the august judgment and the constraining mercy of the Holy of Israel, is involved in this concern. The — so to speak in our deficient human terms — objective Word of God " *burns* " in them as a consuming fire, as Jeremiah has put it. They do not *have* the message. The message *has* them: " O earth, earth, earth, *hear* the word of the Lord " (Jer. 22:29) . The messengership in the New Testament shows the same prophetic temperature in the apostles. Paul is particularly conspicuous in this respect. His proclamation of the gospel, of what God did and does in Jesus Christ, is at the same time an intense confession of faith, a deep conviction which rings through all his words. The apostle John in the opening of his First Letter expresses in a marvelous way this oneness of subjectivity and objectivity: "That which was from the beginning, which we have heard, which we have seen with our eyes, which we have looked upon, and our hands have handled, of the Word of life; . . . that which we have seen and heard declare we unto you, that ye also may have fellowship [koinōnia] with us: and truly our fellowship is with the Father, and with his Son Jesus Christ." One might call these verses the "magna charta" of communication in the Biblical sense. "Communication of" and "communication between," their ground, their purpose and meaning find here a unified expression, because of the adoring awe for the "wonderful works of God." Perhaps it is appropriate to say: in these Johannine words "communication regained" is formulated, which amounts in a certain sense to "paradise regained."

Because Biblical revelation signifies God's self-disclosure to man in his impotence to know God as he really is, communication belongs to the very essence of revelation. Biblically said, God *wants,* God *yearns,* to be known in his being, his will, and his purpose with man and the world. This yearning is the creative background of the strange, mysterious divine drama of self-communication as embodied in God's wrestling with the people of Israel with which he covenanted and in the incarnation, life, death, and resurrection of Christ. This yearning finds its necessary and natural expression in the urge for communication, which inheres in the Church and its members, if the Church understands its true nature, and which we call its missionary obligation or its apostolic mandate.

What has been said up to now, although far too briefly, is the essence of what ought to be said theologically about communication in Biblical light. It would be deeply interesting to enter also in the field of means and methods of communication in Biblical light. The extravagant and nearly exclusive stress on verbal communication, on preaching and sermonizing, in the world of the Churches, which issued from the Reformation, is a degeneration or distortion of the Reformer's rediscovery of the prophetic character and quality of the Word of God. This stress has closed the eyes of the Church to the manifold means of communication which we find in the Bible, which in contradiction to our Western world is not confined to, or imprisoned in, a "verbal culture." The leading idea in elaborating the many Biblical data or allusions to possible means of communication would have to be that of the Bible's natural tendency to take fully seriously the fact of man's wholeness and diversity. One of the important conclusions of such an elaboration would be (as we shall see in our last chapter) that the current conception of communication — that is, how to communicate the gospel in a language that the secular man can understand — as one of the great contemporary problems of the Church is too narrow and one-sided. Of course, this aspect is implied in the problem, but it is only one aspect and probably not the most important for the reason that the Christian message, which must be communicated, has such deep and wide dimensions that they transcend the territory of verbal culture, howsoever refined and high its standard may be. And for another reason also, namely, that the critical and questionable (*fragwürdig*) situation of the Christian Church and message in the world of today must be met by many more and different means than that of more comprehensible language.

Yet, although we have a right to maintain that what we have said is essentially implied in the reality of Biblical revelation in regard to communication, some additional observations of crucial importance are indispensable.

The first observation is that, although, as we indicated, communication is deeply embedded in the nature of Biblical revelation and in the Biblical understanding of God and of man, the communication of the gospel, which is necessarily incumbent upon the Church and its members, is neither primarily nor ultimately dependent on our human ability to communicate. We are perennially called to and (if we really understand our place in God's design) urged toward the desire of communication, and implicitly we are called to a constant sharpening and modifying of our abilities in communication. And nevertheless, throughout the Bible it is consistently maintained that the primary author of the effective transmission of the message is the Holy Spirit. This demonstrates clearly that communication of the gospel has a quality of its own, different from communication as generally understood and on a different level. In other words, communication of the gospel, although it certainly has much in common with the universal phenomenon of communication between men, cannot be regarded as *one* of the many forms of communication. It is a category *sui generis,* at least theologically speaking. It is not simply communication between two partners, but the invisible third partner, the Holy Spirit, is the chief one. The peculiar character and place of communication of the Christian message appears in the fact that its inherent aim is not *persuasion,* however persuasive the act of communication may be, as has to be the case with all communication between men, but *conversion*. " Repent ye, and believe the gospel " (Mark 1:15).

My second additional observation is closely connected with this last word: conversion. Communication is, as follows from all that we have said, the lifeblood of the Church. It is inherent in the message. Persuasive, convincing communication is its great task under all circumstances and situations. The reason that communication has become a great problem is that the Church is experiencing the evident lack of persuasive and convincing power in its presentation of the message, whatever the cause of this fact may be. Hence the search for a more effective presentation and communication, leading toward searching self-examination and untiring efforts to understand the world in which communication must take place.

But once again the Christian message manifests its peculiar character, its specific categorical nature. The Bible tells that it *must* be proclaimed, communicated. This is a matter of the greatest urgency. The search for souls is imperative. But being the message of the cross, of the mysterious wisdom of God, which acts as the saving power of God, precisely for this reason it is a scandal to all self-confident human wisdom. It is not according to, but against, human nature, although it is the only power capable of converting man into his true, God-willed nature. The most fervent apostle and communicator of the gospel is undoubtedly Paul, who bent his whole life in one direction, that is to say, in the direction of becoming everything to all men in order that they might accept the gospel. It is this man who emphasizes the unacceptable, divine foolishness inherent in the message.

What does this imply? It seems to me that it implies the

important indication that the best communication does not necessarily guarantee success. The search for successful communication has no Biblical justification. Only the search for faithful, really interpretative communication has.

My third additional observation is about the Biblical concept of the hardening of hearts. Let us particularly stress the point that this is meant in the Bible as an occurrence from God's side and from man's side. To be frank and honest, this concept, especially when mentioned in the Bible from God's side, is uncongenial to us people of the twentieth century, impregnated as we are with the seemingly benevolent humanitarianism which since the eighteenth century has belonged to the atmosphere in which we breathe. Need I mention the many parts of the Bible where it occurs? For brevity's sake the mentioning of Pharaoh in Exodus, of Psalm Ninety-five and the serious laboring of this point in Heb., chs. 3 and 4, must suffice. This is very pertinent to the treatment of communication in Biblical light. The three examples just mentioned are excellent cases of communication, both between God and man and between man and man. Our Lord freely uses this concept of God hardening the hearts of men as a *result of purposive communication by parables* which by us are usually considered to be models of adaptive communication. Compare e.g., Matt. 13:11–15. As so often, our Lord in this case appeals to the Old Testament, Isa., ch. 6, where in a strangely striking way Isaiah, after having had the vision of God's glory and having offered himself to God in order to be " sent," received as God's message to convey to the people the following one: " Hear ye indeed, but understand *not;* and see ye indeed, but perceive *not* " (Isa. 6:9). This cardio-sclerosis (hardening of heart), also called " fattening of the heart," is according to the Bible an act of God, and it happens. It is, *within* the act of communication, the frustration of communication. We must not close our eyes to it, and still less, in trying to find our way in the problem of communication, should we leave it out of our considerations. It is never wise to neglect an aspect of plain Biblical teaching. This persistent occurrence in the Bible of cardiosclerosis as a negative response to God or as an act of divine judgment points to the " mystery of iniquity " in the world, the realm of demonic power to which man can deliver himself and thus make himself inaccessible to communication of the Christian message. For the third time we have to make the observation that it is in relation to the communication of the Christian message only that the mysterious thing happens: communication as a means of its annihilation. If there is proof for the contention — which is mine — that communication is not only a psychological matter but ultimately a metaphysical or theological matter, it is precisely this fact of cardiosclerosis.

To think and live with the Bible in such a way that our fundamental thinking is inspired and governed by its view of man and the world implies being fully conscious of its dominant motive, that all that happens in and through men in all their relationships and in all the fields of life cannot be really and adequately understood and explained psychologically, sociologically, historically, or economically. To say this sounds very unmodern. It is the pride of our time — and this pride undoubtedly has justification — that by all these new means of analysis and understanding we have made enormous progress. Hence the great prestige of science in our modern world of regulative ideas. Most Christians are in their thinking and approach also under the spell of this idol. In Biblical light, in my opinion, we should not hesitate for a moment, with all due respect to science, to take the position that *notwithstanding* its achievements this way of understanding the mystery of man and the world is ultimately, when used as the *only* " royal " way, a blind alley. The Biblical affirmation is that man is always, in all his ways, under the determining influence of the " bondage under the elements of the world " (Gal. 4:3) and under " principalities and powers " (Eph. 6:12; Rom. 8:38; Col. 2:15), which are never included and cannot be included in the calculations of modern scientific methods of explanation and understanding, because they have their place in the transcendent world of Biblical faith, and not in the immanent world picture of the modern mind. Note that the New Testament — this view runs through the whole New Testament, although I have quoted verses only from Paul's epistles — speaks about slavery (bondage), and counts this bondage as belonging to the state of " immature, nonadult " people (in Greek, *nēpioi*). The Biblical message is that men everywhere must be liberated from this bondage. That is what is literally meant by " redemption " liberation from bondage (Greek, *apolytrōsis*). In this view, in spite of the undeniably liberating forces released by science in all its aspects under the *cultural*, historical angle of view, yet science is ultimately a modern form of idolized bondage.

In this Biblical perspective we get some inkling of the dynamic and tremendous implications of the Lordship of Christ, the great Liberator, and of what " Christian liberty " may mean.

Nevertheless, the Biblical view of communication, as inherent in the nature of revelation as God's *redemptive* purpose with man and the world, remains unimpaired the fundamental tone of the divine melody, because the God who hardens the hearts in certain cases is God our Saviour, "who will have all men to be saved, and to come unto the knowledge of the truth" (I Tim. 2:4), and Jesus, who spoke in parables "because they seeing see *not;* and hearing they hear *not*" (Matt. 13:13), is the Lord, who came to seek and save sinners.

# 2 *Communication in the History of the Church*

THE GOSPEL, THE MESSAGE OF GOD'S SALVATION AND JUDG-
ment, of the coming Kingdom, entered into an indifferent
and hostile world. As such, this is not at all startling or
amazing. Human nature, and especially the spiritual structure of any human society, is conservative, requires conformity, and reacts, to a new phenomenon that does not
seem immediately assimilable, with indifference, diffidence,
and often with some kind of opposition to such an unde-
sired intruder. Of course, only gradually the Roman-Greek
world began to realize that this Christian Church with its
message was not only a new thing, perhaps annoying, perhaps attractive, but was extremely dangerous to the heart
of ancient civilization, and to the whole structure of the
world as it existed in the form of the Roman Empire. Cel-
sus, the first pagan polemicist of whom we have extensive
knowledge, demonstrates this remarkable combination of
aristocratic scorn of this, in his eyes, plebeian uncouth religion of uncouth people, with genuine fear of its flat contradiction of the fundamental bases of pagan society. This
fear sometimes verges on imploring this annoying and disturbing power to be reasonable and conform at least to the
myth of Caesar's divinity, which was the cornerstone of the
Roman Empire.

However, as we know, the expression "indifferent and hostile world" needs some qualification. The world into which the gospel entered was in a mood hungry for salvation, conceived in various terms. It was a hunting field of competing mystery cults, promising and effecting salvation from the ills and evils of existence. In this atmosphere the Christian Church grew up in the first three centuries, and played, from the profane historical point of view, the role of the increasingly successful rival of the great mystery cults, just because it was the only one that was periodically persecuted and stood on the list for liquidation. So there existed "points of contact" in this whole atmosphere. The New Testament, especially the Pauline Epistles, bear evidence to this fact. In looking over the span of the first three centuries, it must be said that one of the main forms of communication has been a far-going attempt at adaptation, result of gradual growth, not of conscious planning and strategy. It is in this sense that in the atmosphere of competition the Christian Church assumed more and more the likeness and fashion of a mystery cult. It was essentially different, however, from the other mystery cults because it enshrined the Biblical religion of faith, with its prophetic, priestly, and pastoral character and genius.

Before we start on our journey through the history of the Church, stopping for lack of time and space only at certain stations to illustrate the vicissitudes of communication, this is the right place for some general remarks in regard to the first three centuries, when the Church was, generally speaking, under the cross. The great extension of the Church happened in the fifty or sixty years before the Diocletian Persecution, the last fierce attempt to oust the Church. The great adventure was that the Church had to communicate a message which in its real purport is "the foolishness of

God," which "destroys the wisdom of the wise" because wiser than men, and which is the "weakness of God, stronger than men"; and is at the same time the "desire of the nations." Therefore, in principle it is incommunicable, it cannot find an adequate translation in any human mode of speech and thought, and yet it touches the deepest aspirations and needs of men, so having in principle also at least a possibility of resonance, of vibration.

The little flock of Jesus entered and lived, however, in a given world, and so the message had to be expressed in terms apprehendable to this world. This obtains the more for Christianity, just because it is the religion of historical facts of salvation with a message concerned about the world and men as they are. In other words, the Church, by nature "the colony of heaven," the people expecting the Kingdom of God, and their Lord, who will come to end the historical drama by judging the quick and the dead, has on its pilgrimage to *establish* itself in the world and develop a structure, a style, a mode of existence. In this, fundamentally speaking, uncommunicable character of the message, which nevertheless is meant to be proclaimed loudly and gladly, and in this history-transcending character of the Church, which nevertheless has to take a body in this historical world, lies the perennial, insoluble tension in which the Church has to live. The deeper the consciousness of the tension and the urge to take this yoke upon itself are felt, the healthier the Church is. The more oblivious of this tension the Church is, the more well established and at home in this world it feels, the more it is in deadly danger of being the salt that has lost its savor.

This peculiar character of the Church, which is called to communication with the world and communication of the message, implies that both aspects of communication plunge

it, from the beginning, into the problem that communication cannot but take the form of expression, adaptation,
assimilation. The Church cannot live without them, and
has to practice them vigorously, not timidly. During its
whole history, also its future history, the Church, therefore,
pends between the Scylla of succumbing in the attempt, or
the Charybdis of shunning the attempt, surrendering itself
in this case to the vain illusion of remaining unspotted of
the world.

In the pages of the New Testament, especially in the
Pauline Epistles (for the simple reason that Paul was in the
first place a missionary and builder of the Church), we immediately find the evidence of this combat. We also find
there the imperishable directives and points of orientation
for this hazardous journey of the ship of the Church. We
shall select some salient points of the encounter of Church
and world in the first centuries, and of the Church's practice of communication, drawing mainly upon A. von Harnack's masterful work: *Die Mission und Ausbreitung des
Christentums in den ersten drei Jahrhunderten* (The Mission and Expansion of Christianity in the First Three Centuries). C. J. Cadoux, *The Early Church and the World,*
as well as other literature, also contains ample information.

The profound difference between the Primitive Church
and our present situation is that the Primitive Church entered as a tiny new thing into a pagan world, inheritor of
a great history, whereas at present Christianity lives as a
still big, but old, institution in a world in whose formative
history it has played a decisive role, but which has now
emancipated itself from the unquestioned authority of and
allegiance to the Church. The resemblance between the
Primitive and the present Church is that then and today
(at least in many parts of the world) the Church is a mi-

nority. There is even ground for maintaining the thesis that in some respects the situation of the Primitive Church was more favorable than the present one. There were external conditions of the Roman-Greek world working in favor of a spread of Christianity and conducive to communication in the two senses we use it in our lectures. There was one empire, one world language, one culture, a common trend toward monotheism, a common nostalgia for saviors, a common feeling that understanding of life, religion, and strong moral discipline belong together. This impressive list is an eye opener to our present destitution.

Harnack summarizes the expansion and communication of Christianity in the following illuminating points: The main points of the missionary proclamation in the first century were: (1) The Kingdom of God is at hand, Jesus the Resurrected is the expected Messiah, the message is the fulfillment of Old Testament revelation (I Cor. 12:2; 15:4, etc.; Acts 13:38, etc.; I Thess. 1:9, etc., give a good idea of the communication of the message). It is very important to note here that in the second century the kerygma had changed considerably. Instead of the elemental tones we hear in the verses just quoted, the main points of emphasis were: the one living God, the Soter and Judge Jesus Christ, the forgiveness of sins, the resurrection of the flesh, continence (in the ancient world this resolute abandonment of the world in the face of divine majesty was revolutionary), all five still challenging enough in the ancient world, but showing a difference of axis with the New Testament. (2) The gospel of the Saviour and of blessing. (3) The battle against the power of the demons. (4) The gospel of love and practical aid. (5) The religion of the Spirit and power, or moral sincerity and sanctification of life. (6) The religion of authority and reason, of the mysteries, and of transcendental knowledge. (7) The message of the new people and the third species, in which the Christian consciousness in regard to history and the field of political life was expressed. (This last point has great relevance for us today.)

Pervading all this, the preaching of severe morality, of a determinate change (*metanoia*), the firm conviction of God's presence and guidance, were strong elements in the total act of communication. Harnack particularly stresses the point that the Christians were entirely new by the fact of their being a strong union of charity and practical aid. In a colossal way the Christian community practiced the rules given at the end of 'Matt., ch. 25. As Harnack says — and this is extremely important for a discussion on communication, which at present is in danger of moving principally on intellectual lines — "The new language of the Christians was the language of love in power and act" (*op. cit.*, 2d ed., p. 173).

Under the most difficult circumstances care for the poor, the sick, those in prison and in exile, was practiced. The Church developed no action or program — to use our modern Church jargon — for the abolition of slavery as a social institution, but it treated them rigorously as equals and of equal value, especially when they became members of the Church. (Slaves could occupy any rank in the clergy, including that of bishop.) Exorcism was a means of manifesting the powers of the Kingdom, because to the Christians the age of Christ was not, as to many of us who have succumbed to the suggestion of modern apprehension of life, an important spiritual and cultural phase in human history, but the new age in which the victorious powers of

God are at work and wrestle with the demonic powers which enslave the world. (This again is extremely relevant to our own situation.)

In all these senses, and in many more, Christianity became a social message of very specific caliber. Harnack rightly points as evidence of its significance to Justinian's imitation-endeavor to restore paganism. Moreover, by its character as a universal brotherhood under Christ, Christianity developed into a center over against the State. In an indirect way the attitude of the martyrs, the personal expression of the Christian way of life by the ordinary members of the Church, mostly simple, unlettered people, the local congregation as a concrete embodiment of the whole Church, possessed a power of communication, often transcending by far all direct and conscious efforts. The study of this whole process of encounter is very illuminating, because on the one hand the means of indirect communication appear numberless, *if there is a faithful allegiance to the new reality in Christ,* and on the other hand it is clear that often the points of attraction, the doors to step in, have their historically conditioned aspects (e.g., the point of greatest attraction often was the promise of " purification " and " eternal life," *the* concerns of the mystery religions) .

It is worth-while to have a look at the struggle with adaptation by paying attention for a moment to the conflicts of Christians in their profession. The great question was, How far is a Christian allowed to enter into the professional jobs of those days with their mores and customs, *without denying Christ and without becoming polluted by participation in idolatry?* In this pagan world, it was indeed a very intricate question. Was it at all possible for a Christian to partake in this utterly pagan society in such a vital sphere as

professional life? This question has been fiercely debated.
There were, of course, different attitudes: rigorous, lax, etc.
Tertullian (e.g., in his *De spectaculis*) has been one of the
most violent partisans of the rigorous party. How to be a
Christian in professional life was a question of life and
death then, just as now: then, in a pagan society; now, in
a secular society with its camouflaged idolatries. It raised
the whole question of the relationship of Church and culture. It was inevitable that there were lists of professions,
untouchable to Christians, as there ought to be now, although quite different. A special point, treated, for instance, by Tertullian, is the question whether within the
framework of the educational school system of the ancient
world a Christian could be a teacher or a professor. His
answer is no, for they get too much immersed in a life and
teaching that are steeped in idolatry. But even the rigorous
Tertullian shows that the problem of the *relation* of Church
and culture is inescapable, and cannot be answered by the
slogan of separation or isolation. Although he forbids
teaching, he allows " learning," making the remarkable
pronouncement: " How can we reject the application to
worldly studies without which the religious studies cannot
exist? " In this battle between the rigorous, the lax, and the
many middle positions, it is important to note that there is
often a very virile tone. To the argument, " I have nothing
to live on if I leave my profession," one sometimes finds the
answer, " A Christian ought not to be afraid of hunger."

Without saying something on the apologetes we cannot
leave the period of the Primitive Church, when the Church,
although establishing itself gropingly in the world, was
never established, but always in principle and often in practice an insecure candidate for ostracism. In the stricter
sense of communication by word they were the people who

consciously sought for communication on the highest level of philosophical and religious discourse and dialogue. The urge for communication inherent in the Biblical message, as we indicated in the first chapter, manifests itself in the work of the apologists. Indirectly this appears in the striking fact that whereas the many mystery religions took a passive attitude toward the religious philosophy of the imperial religion, the Christians engaged in an encounter. In the beginning it was even one-sided. The apologists made their case for the Christian faith, and expressed their estimation of Greek religion and philosophy, often without finding a real partner for a dialogue. Christianity was still too inconspicuous, but the more it grew in weight the more seriously it was taken. This dialogue from both sides certainly did not exemplify ideal communication as the phenomenology of communication now defines it. Rather, it showed, because it was in fact a combat, all the marks of mutual misunderstanding and mutual misinterpretation which are the usual concomitants of communication in concrete life of all ages. In the present time we feel more deeply the frustrations of these defects because the fundamental principles of democracy and science have developed, at least in a tiny minority, a more acute feeling for the necessity of genuine mutual understanding in the process of communication. The apologetes were in many cases eager to meet their opponent by giving to Roman-Greek culture and religion a certain place in the scheme of divine revelation. They were, moreover, often unconsciously still so strongly enchanted by the fundamental notions of the culture to which they belonged that their presentation of the faith was often an adaptation, which fell far short of the Biblical message and was what is called in our time a reduction of this message.

With Constantine the great change came. In the time preceding the Edict of Milan (312) Christianity had proved able to become the religion of the subjects of the empire, but it was Constantine's *political* decision to declare it the most favored religion of this world state in transition which made Christianity the molding social and spiritual power of the future. The time of the great temptation began. It became the task of the Church, as an instrument in the hand of the State, to Christianize a world, which meant at the same time to secularize itself, to become worldly. It is not our duty to enter into this process, but we can confine ourselves to a few points which are essential to the problem of communication from then on. The first point is that the message, the faith, although in themselves remaining, and in many personal cases operating, according to their true nature, undergo an important change of position in the whole context of the life of the empire. They become the *ideology* of an empire in transition, the bond of social, political, and cultural cohesion. The symphonia, to use the official orthodox theological term, of faith and empire, of Church and State, is consequently the ideal conception of the best possible form of living together of Church and State. In fact, when put in the light of the prophetic message of Biblical revelation, it is a surrender of the tension, inherent and necessary in the relation of Christian faith and world, about which we spoke. Here lies the root of the marriage between nationalism and Christianity, which is peculiar to all orthodox countries where orthodoxy is paramount.

The second point is that in this new stage of the Church's career, the development of rigid doctrinal formulation began. Orthodoxy in the full sense of the word was born. In itself, doctrinal formulation is, in the historical career of a religion, a wholesome and indispensable necessity, and we are accustomed to look from a great distance at these formative doctrinal controversies mainly under that angle. At that time, however, and also for future generations, they meant also something else and something more, and this " else " and " more " obtained prominence. That is to say, they functioned in fact as the creed of an ideology of a religious-social structure, which is a relative historical phenomenon, but which through the ideology was absolutized. One of the main consequences of this development was that the self-consciousness of Christianity became pre-eminently doctrinal, which is not in accordance with the hidden symphony of emphases in the Biblical message. Only in this light does the attitude and judgment of the Christian Church toward other religions and toward " heresy " in the closing period of the ancient world — " *die christliche Spätantike* " as the Germans say, in the Middle Ages, and also in various grades after the Reformation — become understandable. Other religions and heresies were felt either as rival ideologies or as diabolic inventions, attacks on the established social and political order. Combined with this feeling of enmity, there remained a line of thinking which gave to other religions some kind of place in the plan of God's revelation, as we have already remarked; but this did not change the strong emphasis on the doctrinal. Hence the preponderance of denunciatory, anathematizing, invective language, which strikes us moderns so much. One cannot often enough say that this was sincerely meant, because the faith in the ideology and its creed, which was the Christian creed, was so sincere. This central doctrinal Christian self-consciousness has had disastrous consequences for communication, " communication between " as well as " communication of." The only field where, within the framework of the primacy of the doctrinal, greater latitude was taken was that of missions.

In a certain sense, the last example of communication in the deepest and widest sense of the word has been in the last, Christian period of antiquity the lifework of Augustine. Ernst Troeltsch in his *Augustin, die christliche Antike und das Mittelalter* (Augustine, Christian Antiquity and the Middle Ages) has, in my opinion, shown this in a masterful fashion by the way in which he characterizes Augustine's *De civitate Dei* as the first great "ethics of culture" of Christianity. Augustine, who was a rhetor and literate before he became a Christian, wrought in an eye-to-eye struggle with the gospel, out of his life experience, a feasible but *knowingly precarious* * synthesis of the Christian faith and ancient culture. He tried to incorporate the world — which was to him, of course, the ancient world — and its relative goods and values into an ethics of the *summum bonum*, i.e., God or absolute being in whom truth, beauty, and goodness coalesce. But he maintained the gulf between *Civitas Dei* and *terrena* (the Celestial City and the earthly city). Because of this precariousness he became in the Middle Ages the starting point of many divergent currents, and in the Roman Catholic Church the voice that often called the Church back to more Biblical emphases.

We shall give some examples of both the frustration of communication and the latitude which it developed in missions. The greatest challenge and danger that the

* By "knowingly precarious" I mean that Augustine was conscious of the hazardousness of the undertaking and the many awkward questions or the ambiguous character of many solutions that remained. A testimony to this consciousness of the precarious character of his grandiose attempt is one of his last books, *Retractiones*. Compare also C. N. Cochrane, *Christianity and Classical Culture,* particularly the last chapter.

Church had to sustain in the days of the Byzantine Empire was the appearance of Islam on the stage of history. Everybody knows that a considerable part of Christian territory, in North Africa and the Near East, became Moslem. As far as the Christian Church continued to exist, it did so as a protected minority, forced back into a certain ghetto, but with legal status. By its gallant resistance Byzantium was during ages the wall of protection for Europe against a Moslem invasion. One must fully take into account this situation in order to have a fair judgment of the fact that the relations of the Christian and the Moslem world, in spiritual respect, have been so distressingly sterile. Islam is *by its nature* the ideology of a cultural, social, and political system, and met as its opponent a Christendom, which also behaved, *against the nature of the Christian faith,* as the ideology of a cultural, social, and religious system. Meeting each other in any real sense was, therefore, impossible. In the many apologetical and polemical skirmishes from both sides, moreover, communication in any sense was nonexistent because the tone was determined by this objective situation and by a doctrinal bias, which had become second nature. The debate could never become a discourse. It remained a sterile mock fight of two monologues. There are in the Middle Ages exceptional men, like Raimundus Lullus and Francis of Assisi, who set their heart on converting the Moslems for the love of Christ, and not on confounding enemies. They really tried to communicate. But they were bound to remain lonely figures within the structure and mood of both religions and civilizations.

The second example we take from the field of how heresy was treated. It is logical that with the preponderance of doctrinal judgment in a society for which the authoritative doctrines are not only the creed of the Church but the ideological basis of society heresy is a deadly danger. As a rule it was therefore not possible to see heretics in the first place as erring sheep of the flock, or as people, who by their opinions, attitude, and criticism constituted a partly justified criticism of the Church. Communication was, therefore, in principle, not possible; only refutation, excommunication, or liquidation. Bernard of Clairvaux, who used in his days his last forces to meet the heretics, acted consistently on the thesis that they ought to be overcome by persuasion and not by violence. Yet his pattern of persuasion properly belonged to the category of refutation, but refutation in which the concern for souls was active. All three — refutation, excommunication, and liquidation —have happened.

In the Middle Ages the conflict of the Church with Cathari and Waldensians affords a clear illustration. The spread of these heresies from Italy to Holland was a real menace to the Church and its authority. It must also be seen against the background of the extreme worldly deterioration of many parts of the Church. The Cluniacensian reforms and other movements were serious, and partly successful, attempts at betterment from within the Church. The heretics, in fact, brought a rival Church into being, founded on a dualistic (and certainly heretical) conception of man, a fierce emphasis on poverty as the only adequate Christian way of life — which was in fact a vehement protest against the absolutistic theocratic pretensions of a worldly and dissolute Church — and an indiscriminate criticism of doctrines and rites of the Church, particularly of those that had a great place in popular religion (indulgences, purgatory, Masses for the dead, etc.) . What was to be done with such people who, in a society which was so closely identified with the Church and the Church with society, could not but appear as subversive, criminal forces? In such a situation communication, even in its most distorted or degraded form, was hardly possible. It is interesting to note how things developed. In 1022 the first public act of repression of Catharism happened at the initiative of *secular* government. King Robert the Pious, of France, condemned at Orléans the Cathari for the first time. The mob played a great role in his condemnation of these enemies of society. The Church then demanded only excommunication. This had two reasons: First, canonical law did not know of any other punishment or retribution in such severe cases. Secondly, various voices of the leading clergy showed great diffidence against physical violence and forced compliance, being aware of the law of charity as proclaimed by the gospel.

Gradually, the hesitancy caused by the better conscience of the peculiar character of the Christian faith disappeared. In the face of the growing power of heresy and its frank attack on the institutional Church as an ally of Satan, the creed of the indissoluble unity of Church and society gained the upper hand, or, to use our previous formula, the principle of ideology threw the principle of faith into the background. The Inquisition, or to employ contemporary terms, the Tscheka, of the Church was born. As we know, it did everything belonging to the Tscheka, except the execution of the final capital punishment, which was left to the secular arm. In a certain sense, the Church, by its official recognition and use of the newly arisen mendicant orders, acknowledged in a hidden way the criticism against its secularization, but in fact the Dominicans became the instruments par excellence of the Inquisition with all its horrors. We have intentionally dwelt on this development in order to clarify the point why communication, i.e., a real dialogue of Church and heresy, was impossible, although the demand for it lies in the nature of the Christian faith.

It is worth-while to note that it was secular government which began with violent repression. This was quite logical, because these heretics undermined the bases of existing society of which this government was the symbol and guardian. The Church wavered in following, because the consciousness of the spirit of the gospel still put some repressive pressure on its ideological consciousness of being the soul of a totalitarian, God-willed society. The ideological flood, however, broke the weak dikes of Christian sensitivity, and the campaign of merciless repression started under the leadership of the Church. Bernard of Clairvaux, as already noted, was one of the few who in the midst of the fury tried to follow the way of persuasion. " *Capiantur non armis, sed argumentis* " (" They must be taken not by arms, but by arguments ") was his motto, but even he sadly succumbed to the doubt whether it was, after all, not better to deliver the heretics to the mercies of secular government in order to avoid endangering the salvation of the souls of the orthodox flock. If one analyzes this, it is clear that in Bernard's soul the pastoral motive and the " doctrinal " bent of mind we have already characterized combined to achieve his reluctantly given assent to the policy of violent suppression by the Inquisition. It is the same drama which happened to Augustine, the great refuter of the Donatists, who finished with the fierce appeal, expressed in his phrase *compelle intrare,* i.e., compel to enter (the Church) .

For a balanced judgment it is indispensable to take the historical situation fully into account. " Judge not, that ye be not judged " (Matt. 7:1) is the injunction of our Lord, also applicable in this case. But it is as indispensable to say that, in the light of the true nature of the Christian faith, it is a tragedy to see such great Christians as Augustine and Bernard in their perplexity in an overwhelmingly difficult situation succumbing to the identification of faith and totalitarian ideology, although even then they certainly were not oblivious of the true genius of faith. In regard to our subject, this excursus was necessary because it exemplifies the tragedy of complete breakdown of communication *within* the Church in its treatment of heresy. The parallels with our own time of totalitarianisms, avowed or unavowed, are inescapable. The chief difference with the Church is that the Church acted totalitarian with a bad conscience; pagan or pseudo-religious or nihilist totalitarianisms did and do it with a good conscience.

Above, we spoke of the greater latitude, often apparent in missions, in regard to the efforts toward real " communication between " and "communication of." The perennial problem of missions is that of communication. Missions is one of the great training grounds of the Church in communication. In our days, by the totally new situation in which Christian missions and the Churches in the so-called non-Christian countries are thrown, communication has become anew a burning problem. Every new situation requires its reinterpretation. The Churches in the West and the Churches in the non-Christian countries will do well to co-operate very closely on the problem of communication, and they can learn much from each other. However, we must refrain from dealing specifically with the problem of communication in the present missionary situation, not only because for the moment we are dealing with the problem of communication in the history of the Church, but also because it would require a rather voluminous book to treat it adequately.

From among the many examples available in history, we

select again a few, taken from the expansion of Christianity by Roman-Catholic missions. We do so on purpose, in order to demonstrate the latitude about which we spoke within the framework of a preponderantly doctrinal estimation of religions, and, in particular, of Christian truth. What is the theological basis for this latitude, if not always in fact, at any rate in theory? The fundamental conception of Christianity as the only true and perfect religion over against the false and imperfect religions always had a complement, generally expressed in various shades of the theologoumenon of the activity of the Logos in all religions, which show vestiges of this activity but are concretely mainly degenerations caused by human corruption. Another approach is the vindication of the so-called best elements in non-Christian religions by the doctrine of natural religion as a preceding stage to revealed religion. This last form has received its clearest formulation in the system of Thomas Aquinas, which is for all practical purposes and intentions canonized by the Church. It has become the fertile basis for all misionary communication attempts of the Roman Catholic Church. But before the systematization by the Aquinate, these currents of Logos and natural religion concepts in a more loose form pervaded the attitude of the Church in missionary situations, as a heritage of the apologetes and the Apostolic Fathers. This theological background is the cause of the fact that the problem of communication was not primarily a concern for the faithful and living transmission of the Biblical faith, with the highly dialectical consequences to which this leads, but rather for the transmissal of the body of revealed verities combined with a strategy of adaptation and assimilation in a new cultural and spiritual environment. To put it sharply, not so much the message must be proclaimed, but the Church as a keeper of infallible truth and as a hierarchical institution must be transplanted. (This formula needs qualification, for the discussion of which there is no room. But essentially I hold it as true and exact. It would be fascinating also to weigh critically Protestant missions in this light. We still need a Biblical theology of missions.)

The first example we adduce is the Christianizing of England through the missionary band of Augustine, the first Roman Catholic Archbishop of Canterbury (cf. K. S. Latourette, *A History of the Expansion of Christianity,* Vol. II, pp. 36 ff., and Bede, *Ecclesiastical History of the English Nation,* Everyman's Library, Book I, Chs. XXII to XXXII). In 596, Pope Gregory I, called the Great, sent a group of Benedictine monks from Rome on a missionary errand to England, under the leadership of Augustine, the head of the monastery of which Gregory himself had been abbott. During the journey, in Gaul, the brethren grew terrified by the dangers and hardships of the undertaking. Augustine went to Rome for new instructions. It is a marvelous letter Gregory gave to Augustine as a reply to the brethren. It is a Christian letter, in the deepest sense of the word, full of truly fraternal kindness, but ordering them to persevere faithfully and fearlessly. The conversion of King Ethelbert of Kent and of his people had certainly much to do with the prestige of Rome, then decaying but still surrounded by the unforgettable glory of the world empire of the past. As so often in the Middle Ages — and also in modern missions among primitive peoples — the tribe followed the king because he was the keystone and symbol of the old order, and by his conversion inaugurated the new order. The political and religious are intertwined. After the decisive step of the king, education in Christianity began. Education means adaptation, assimilation, and only partly iconoclasm.

It also meant social, often even economic, education, solicitude for the poor and the slaves. All this played its part
in " communication between " and " communication of."
The most noteworthy document of adaptation, full of sa-
gacity, is another letter of Gregory (see Bede, Vol. I,
Ch. XXX). He urges in this letter not to destroy the pagan
temples, but only the idols in them; then, after having
sprinkled the temples with holy water, to erect altars, place
relics, and so convert them " from the worship of devils to
the service of the true God." The old pagan slaughter of
oxen as sacrifices cannot be continued, but the nativities of
the holy martyrs should be celebrated at the former temples by religious feasting, and by killing cattle to the praise
of God. Gregory's motivation of these and similar advices
is: " For there is no doubt that it is impossible to efface
everything at once from their obdurate minds, because he
who endeavors to ascend to the highest place rises by degrees or steps, and not by leaps." Communication is through
education and gradual initiation.

A second example of the accommodation of Christianity
to a new alien world is the arduous, fascinating work of the
Jesuit missionary fathers in India and China. This endeavor, which was a gigantic and incredibly persevering attempt at communication in its two senses, lasted with many
vicissitudes about 150 years, from the end of the sixteenth
century until the middle of the eighteenth century. It gave
rise to the famous rites controversy, and finished with the
bull of Pope Benedict XIV, " *Omnium sollicitudinum* " of
September 12, 1744. This bull confirmed all former con-
demnations and restrictions of this accommodation experiment, and commanded its definite stop. The great inaugu-
rators of this experiment were Robert de Nobili in India
and Matteo Ricci in China, not to mention the many other

illustrious names connected with it.

Why did these men conceive such a daring enterprise? On the one hand they were deeply dissatisfied with the poor results of preceding missionary labors. On the other hand they realized that the little that was achieved was a sterile *corpus alienum* in the body of great, magnificent, and self-conscious religious civilizations, many centuries older than Christianity itself. Their problem became: how to penetrate into these citadels, and conquer them from within. Their answer was: combine competent knowledge of these civilizations with a resolute system of accommodation of the Church to the dominant patterns of life and thinking. Their intention was not so much to harmonize the doctrine of the Church with the elemental feeding religious ideas of India and China, although they easily overlooked many insuperable contrasts by detecting in China's and India's spiritual heritage resplendent ground plans of natural religion. They maintained the unchangeableness of the infallible dogma of the Church. What they most eagerly sought was a genuinely Sinicized and Indianized Catholic Church. (The literature about this stupendous adventure is vast. It may suffice to say that the Jesuit fathers by their books, their reports, their "*Lettres édifiantes et curieuses,*" etc., have deeply influenced the European world. Compare, for example, for some information, Henri de Lubac, *La Rencontre du bouddhisme et de l'occident,* Paris, 1952.)

It is neither possible nor necessary to describe these experiments and their repercussions in China, at Rome, and in Europe. The main thing is to signalize them as the most courageous and tenacious attempts ever made at communication on a Roman Catholic basis. This qualification " on a Roman Catholic basis " means that communication is sought through the well-thought-out method of accommo-

dation, which does not even shun great distortions of the
Christian message, *provided the Church be established* in
such an inhospitable soil. This is, of course, a very one-
sided form of communication. One can even say that communication, mainly by accommodation, is not, properly
speaking, communication, but " *pénétration pacifique.*" But
it was meant as the strategy of communication. The final
condemnation after intermittent periods of approbation
had many causes, but the chief ones were an underestima-
tion of the terrific strength of these Oriental civilizations in
their period of undisturbed existence, and the insight that
this, in principle, limitless accommodation would mean the
surrender of the substance of the Church as an infallible,
authoritative institution.

Some remarks have to be made on the nineteenth century
in the light of communication, because then the forces were
in operation which led to what is called, at least in Europe, the breakdown of communication. In later chapters
we shall pay special attention to these aspects. By way of
transition we offer here some preliminary observations.

In the nineteenth century the Church in Europe lost more
and more its central position. In fact, it became a collection of religious associations for the sustenance of individual religious life. The Christian faith, almost exclusively
conceived as a conglomerate of dogmas scandalizing to reason, was constantly under attack. The dazzling discoveries
of science and technics fascinated the minds, and created a
new picture of the world (*Weltbild*), which was mistakenly
taken as the normative " *Weltbild* " forever, a fallacy which
some scientists themselves have dropped now. The *Weltbild*
of the Bible compared as childish and ridiculous with the
new vision. So Bible and Church, by these and many more
causes, lost authority, diminished in function, and had little

power of communication. The glorious era of the future would be, so it was and is often still believed, that of endless progress, the power of man to create an ideal world, the disappearance of dogmatic religion — for the general feeling was that religion is by definition dogmatic — and the advent of the magnificent liberty of the human spirit. Quite in contrast with former centuries, the heretic became the most popular person in the world. (Read G. K. Chesterton's profound and witty criticism of this modern whim, found in his *Heretics*.) The so-called traditional orthodox believer was, and often still is, considered an obscurant. The Church in its orthodox wing got out of touch with the real world of today by its anxiety and inability to interpret and translate. The Church in its liberal wing honestly tried to keep contact and pace with the modern world. The Church reinterpreted the gospel, however, not in accordance with its true meaning, but in its attempt at communication the Church took its cue from the leading ideas of the day. In the name of communication, of preserving the essence and changing the form — as if the correlation of form and content were a simple chemical fact — the pit and strength of the message were diluted. The endeavor, although sincere, did not stop in any way the rising flood of dechristianization. Only a few prophetic men saw through this situation and gave a new powerful interpretation of the Christian message in all its sharpness. They moved on a level above orthodox and liberal, but were not heard by any camp, whether religious or irreligious. It is a significant fact of our time that the great humanists of today, whether they represent the easy, superficial rationalism and idealism which appeals to the present mind, or something deeper, are readily accepted as the authentic leaders of mankind. Theologians, however, who possess at least the same erudition and the same grasp of the problem of life, and who are thinkers of outstanding ability, have no chance whatever of getting the same attention and publicity as the humanists. This is not to complain of, but one must see it in its significance. It is symbolic of the fact that the Christian Church and Christian thinking are, in the general opinion, not really considered respectable, that is to say, worthy of respect. This is one of the hidden difficulties in the problem of communication today. It is obvious that there are no short-cut ways to change this situation. Nor is there reason for desolation, because in many corners of the world, in conspicuous and inconspicuous quarters, the Word of God is on the march " to build and to plant, to destroy and throw down " (cf. Jer. 1:10).

# 3 *Psychological,*
## *Sociological, and Cultural Factors*

IN QUOTING ROGER MEHL IN OUR FIRST CHAPTER, WE SAID
that communication is the fundamental human fact. His
booklet, which grew out of a course on communication that
he gave during the third semester of the Graduate School
for Ecumenical Studies at the Ecumenical Institute, Bossey,
Switzerland, bears the significant title *La Rencontre de
l'autrui* (The Encounter with the Other). There is in the
numerous human situations, which are possible and which
become real, an endless variety of kinds of communication.
Many of them are superficial and casual, but in most cases
some kind of mutual *contact* is sought. Communication
achieves its real intention when it becomes *rencontre de
l'autrui,* encounter with the other, a meeting from eye to
eye and from heart to heart. This ideal encounter, which
is the true meaning and intended aim of communication,
is in fact a rare occurrence between men, and a priceless
experience. The fields where the greatest possibilities of
communication in the full sense of the word are realized are
that of friendship, of the unity of man and wife in marriage, of the authentic community of the fellowship of
believers as the Body of Christ. Life is mostly filled with fail-
ing, frustrated, thwarted, or partly succeeding communication. We ventured to indicate the fundamental religious

reason of this undeniable fact of human existence in our first chapter. In this Biblical light it is understandable why, as intelligent self-observation tells us, communication between men is so often surrounded with mystery. We reach out toward each other, yet do not reach each other. Precisely in relations of real mutual love and trust, as, for instance, in the life of a married couple, this touch of mystery often strikes us. (It is illuminating that the Bible uses for the deepest form of mutual communication, i.e., the sexual union of man and wife, the word "know." This usage connotes the essentially spiritual intent implied in this act.) The point of the ultimate aloneness of either person is reached and demands full respect and consideration, just for the cause of *right* communication which knows its limits. Besides this fundamental religious reason which is behind the various kinds of frustration and of partial success in communication, there are many other secondary, though extremely important, factors which mold and determine communication between men: psychological, cultural, sociological. In this chapter we devote our main attention to some of these factors as a basis for our essential concern: the communication of the Church with the world, or *between* the Church and the world, and the communication *of* the Christian message in and to the world of today.

Before we enter upon this journey, some preliminary remarks have to be made. When calling these psychological, cultural, and sociological factors secondary, we do not intend to assign to them a subordinate role. They are secondary in the hierarchy of factors if we accept — and this is our contention — that the fundamental religious factor is primary throughout, *whether it is recognized or not* and also in the sense that they are disguised manifestations of the fundamental religious reason. In other words, the *theological* estimate ranks first because it uncovers the hidden roots. However, they are not secondary in the ordinary welter of life. There they are prominent and demonstrable to everyone who has eyes to see and ears to hear. It is the universal level where people of different assumptions and convictions can meet each other and enter into discourse. It is one of the benefits of modern times that these factors are not only the field of sagacious observations of able moralists and diagnosticians of the human heart and of human relationships as in the past, but also objects of patient and laborious scientific research. It is legitimate to say that in many cases a too immediate recourse to the fundamental theological reality behind the drama of human communication, coupled with a neglect of these secondary factors, is a damaging simplification and a cause of complete breakdown of communications between Christian thinkers and the world. As in all things, one must be theological at the right moment, and not at every moment, which is a great art.

The custom in the Western countries, and in that part of the world where the Christian Church in its missionary work meets with the great non-Christian religions, to speak of the problem of communication is evidence of an attitude that differs from that of a rather recent past. In this recent past the word "approach" was in vogue. The approach to Hinduism, to Communism, to secular Humanism, etc., were much-treated subjects. By no means has the word "approach" died out, but "communication" is now more fashionable. Although the last has been substituted for the first in many cases, they do not cover the same realm of meaning. The important difference is that "approach" expresses the attitude of the outsider, who tries to find an entrance into an alien world and thus to establish some sort of contact. "Communication" implicitly confesses a given solidarity, taking one's stand *in* the world and as part *of* the world of the other, not over against that world, howsoever sympathetic this may be meant.

This transition from "approach" to "communication" denotes, therefore, a highly important change of orientation which is taking place in many thinking people in the Church. It contains not only a noteworthy modification in understanding of what "communication between" means, but can also have interesting consequences for the understanding of "communication of," that is to say, communication of the Christian message in the present world.

In our days "communication" is a subject that enjoys great interest. As so often (compare, for instance, the vogue of psychology and sociology), this interest testifies to a deep-seated disease in the fabric of human society. The main reason is the predicament of our time and our generation. We go through a colossal breakdown of communication, of possibility of real discourse. To mention only a few examples: in the political field, East and West do not and cannot understand each other. Their discourse, in so far as it exists, is mainly a discourse of mutes. The high rate of divorce in many parts of Western society is another realm of life in which distortion of the ability for communication certainly is one of the causes. In our next chapter we shall, however, turn to a more deliberate evaluation of this breakdown. Existentialist philosophy, which is in some respects a symptom and a response to the predicament in which our generation finds itself, shows a special concern for the theme of "communication." This is logical. This type of philosophy is pervaded by a deep feeling of the aloneness and loneliness or solitariness of man, and puts man in his existential anxieties in the center of its think-

ing. It has, for the first time, created a phenomenology of
" communication " and in doing so has revealed its being
fundamental in the human structure. Karl Jaspers, one of
the outstanding existentialists, manifests in all his works,
without any exception, a deep concern about " communication." To him, in our day in which we lack a *" commune
mesure "* and a " validity of a common mind," communication is an indispensable condition of man's existence
(cf. Jaspers, *Der philosophische Glaube*). Sometimes he
even calls it " the main theme of philosophy " and in his
chief work, *Philosophie,* he has devoted a substantial part
to a penetrating discussion of his view of communication.
To him it is so precious that, although he abhors " the
claim for exclusive truth " of Christianity, he more than
once implores in moving tones the theologians, who in his
eyes are the crusaders of this abominable " claim for exclusive truth," to leave the door open for communication between philosophy and theology.

Roger Mehl, whose booklet we have mentioned twice,
presents us with an excellent phenomenology of communication, the fruit of a marriage of Christian and existentialist
thinking.

We all know that language is the chief, though by no
means the sole, instrument of communication between men,
whether these attempts at communication are successes or
failures. We do not all know and sufficiently realize the
high and mysterious place which language has in human
life. It is perfectly possible to treat the history of human
thinking as a history of the attempts to define the meaning
of language and of the word, and it would, moreover, be
fascinating and revealing to do so. In all ages and great cultures (especially Greek, Indian, and Chinese cultures)
thinkers have meditated upon the place, meaning, and func-

tion of language, but there never was a time like the last
one hundred and fifty years in which we have accumulated
such a vast knowledge about language and languages
through the labors of great linguists, psychologists, and
thinkers. With the characteristic scientific temper of the
modern age the individual and social function of language
has been brought to light. In the following observations,
apart from my own long experience in the field of linguistic
research, I thankfully acknowledge my indebtedness to the
works of two thinkers — no linguists themselves, but philosophers — i.e., the American W. H. Urban, *Language and
Reality* (to avoid misunderstanding we wish to state that
we do not identify ourselves with his realistic ontology
coupled with a horror of all nominalism and his defense of
a *philosophia perennis,* founded on the time-honored sub-
ject-predicate and substance-attribute assumptions as re-
sponding to reality), and the Frenchman G. Gusdorf, *La
Parole.* With the last work especially I am agreeing to a
high extent. Urban rightly urges that language is, ideally
speaking, above all meaningful communication and, therefore, a basal problem of philosophy. The philosophy of
language is to him the philosophy of symbolism. In our
opinion, this basic significance of the meaning, function,
possibilities, limits, and deficiencies of language is too often
overlooked by philosophers as well as by theologians in
their reflections about truth and our human calling and
limitations in regard to it.

Before pursuing the problem of language with regard to
communication, which is of crucial importance to the
Church because of its commission " to preach the Word,"
we should for a moment ask what the Bible, this unphilo-
sophical book, has to say about the word and about language. Indisputably, the " word " is one of the pivotal con-

cepts in the Bible. God creates the world by the power of his " Word." This must not be taken only as a poetical or anthropomorphic expression about which fact, once it has been stated, all is said and done; on the contrary, it has a profound ontological meaning, pointing to the metaphysical background of language in human life. " And God said " introduces every act of creation in Gen., ch. 1. " By the word of the Lord were the heavens made "; " He spake, and it was done; he commanded, and it stood fast " (Ps. 33:6, 9). " Through faith we understand that the worlds were framed by the word of God " (Heb. 11:3). Again, this is not simply explained by calling this poetic phraseology. It goes to the heart of reality. Its deepest foundation is in the Johannine Prologue, where God's supreme and fully authentic act of revelation, Jesus Christ, is the divine Word (" and the Word was God ") and " all things were made by him." This concept is not exclusively Johannine, as is thought so often, but runs through the whole New Testament, reaching back to the famous passages in Proverbs and Job about the divine wisdom.

It would require more than one full chapter to follow up this marvelous subject of the Word in the Bible, where " *mythos* " (originally meaning " word " just as " *logos* ") and " *logos*," which at the dawn of Greek philosophical thinking entered into a never-ending enmity, live in peaceful unity, and to trace the kindred thinking in great and comparatively unknown civilizations that developed around the " Word " as a primeval power. Precisely this universal speculation around the " word " indicates the peculiar place of language in the fabric of human existence, and forbids us to look at it merely as a remarkably useful instrument of intercourse. In other words, as we have observed before, though language is a psychological and social phenomenon, which as such deserves close scrutiny, it is primarily a theological and philosophical problem. This is already expressed in the facts that the really significant difference between man and animal is that " man is a speaking animal " and " the animal lacks only, indeed, the word " (Gusdorf, *op. cit.*, pp. 2, 3) , and that one who is born a deaf mute becomes spiritually and intellectually disintegrated if no means are found to substitute the instrument of language. In the Bible, language means *dialogue,* in the first place dialogue between God and man. And, as we demonstrated in the first chapter, if this divine-human dialogue is broken and disturbed, the dialogue between man and man is in disorder. In other words, language, that marvelous sign of mankind's nobility, becomes a problem full of inner contradictions.

The Bible expresses this important fact in the famous tale of the confusion of languages and the Tower of Babel. This tale of Gen., ch. 11, told in extraordinarily vivid mythological style, is not simply a naïve story, either ridiculous or impressive, according to the individual taste of the sophisticated intellectual mind; it is one of the basic and universal documents of the mysterious drama of man, one of the representative pronouncements on the human existential situation. It revolves around Gen. 11:1: " And the whole earth was of one language, and of one speech," and v. 7: " Let us go down, and there confound their language, that they may not understand one another's speech." This tale and the ideas underscoring it stand in direct sequence to Gen., chs. 1 and 3 about the unhampered dialogue as the hallmark of *normal* human existence in the real sense of the word " normal," and the broken dialogue (between God and man, and between men and men) as the crux of man's *actual* existence. The act of God's verdict and judg-

ment on man is behind its: " Let us go down, and . . . "
But, as the Bible is the record of the acts of God's revelation toward the *re*-creation, the *re*-storement of man in his
*normal* (from the divine point of view) existence, the indispensable complement of Gen., ch. 11 is Acts, ch. 2. In
this last chapter the condition of language in human life
appears to be of paramount significance, because, when the
full power of the Holy Spirit reigns, in other words, when
the divine-human dialogue is restored, the confusion of
languages disappears and there is full communication
again. Fall and redemption, Babel and Pentecost are the
hidden factors behind language and communication. The
story of Acts, ch. 2, indicates with the realism which is peculiar to the Bible the fact that mankind, since this event
of Pentecost, remains pending between fall and redemption,
Babel and Pentecost, because of its own attitude of lack of
faith. " And they were all amazed and marveled " (Acts 2:7)
and again, with a significant change in accent in v. 12:
" And they were all amazed, *and were in doubt*." Once
again, Acts, ch. 2, is not simply a moving or grand story
which stirs the imagination. In it the metaphysical background of mankind's obscure pilgrimage breaks forth. At
the same time it embodies the manifesto of God's sovereign
governance of human history and a secret universal dream
of mankind entering into real historical existence.

A short look at the role of language in philosophical
thinking excellently illustrates the potent impotence of this
dream and bears witness to the words quoted from Acts 2:7
and 12. In order to do this more effectively, we call attention to another aspect of the role of language as it emerges
in the Bible, and appears to give in its naïve way the fundamental religious setting for a problem which has exercised the minds of the greatest thinkers through all the

ages. In Gen., ch. 2, God brings to Adam "every beast of the field, and every fowl of the air . . . to see what he could call them: and whatsoever Adam called every living creature, that was the name thereof" (v. 19). Adam gives the appropriate names. Through the whole Bible the name of God can be taken as God *tout court*. The theme of the "new name" which will be given to those who have received a new life in God or in Christ is running through the whole Bible. "Thou shalt not take the name of the Lord thy God in vain" is a divine commandment, not meant as a prohibition to curse, but as a prohibition to use and exploit God himself for our own ends, because the name and the named are one. To baptize in the name of Jesus Christ is to baptize someone in Christ, into communion with him. So real is the name; so far removed is the name or the word from being a label that can be hung onto things according to our individual and collective whims. In other, more philosophical language: Language and reality are, or should be, intimately or organically connected. Man conquers reality by words, by language. "The arrival of the word manifests the sovereignty of man. Man places between the world and himself the mass of words and so becomes the master of the world." (Cf. G. Gusdorf, *op. cit.*, p. 6.)

What, in the field of philosophical thinking, do we see of that mode of thinking which, in most cases, excludes the relevance of revelation and so differs fundamentally in that respect from the Bible, which puts revelation first? We see that, in spite of this elimination of revelation as the essential factor in reality, it is labored by themes that are treated in the Bible as basic determining factors.

Let us leave for a moment the historical range of our own culture, and look at China. Confucius was so deeply imbued with the idea of the intimate connection between language or word and reality that he brought his whole enterprise of moral, social, and religious reconstruction under the term " the rectifying of names." It was his deep conviction that order and disorder, equilibrium and disequilibrium of the universe, and, therefore, of nature and of social and moral life, hinges on the right or wrong names and words. Under this heading one can profitably treat the whole field of Chinese philosophical thinking and culture. More than one great emperor tried to establish a new peaceful social and political order by the same method of " rectifying the names." In our modern jargon we would say: to establish a basic ideology, a " social myth," for a new system of life. With this important difference, however, that these Chinese emperors believed that in giving, as they said, the appropriate name to everything, they performed a metaphysical act, whereas the modern constructors of " social myths " know that their myths are human inventions, which they, nevertheless, brazenly proclaim as divine injunctions.

Since Socrates started the career of Western philosophical metaphysical thinking by his ironic inquiry into the meaning of words, the philosophy of language has been, expressed or unexpressed, a dominant theme in its development. The famous medieval controversy between realism, conceptualism, and nominalism centered around the question whether language had to be regarded as purely ontological, or whether nihilism or a middle station between ontology and nihilism is the right answer to the fundamental and perennial philosophical problem of the relation of knowing and being. Different philosophies are different " words." It is a matter of life and death for a society whether these different " words " are warring each other, or can maintain a certain harmony within the scope of a common orbit.

The dissolution of the spiritual oneness of the Western world, which had already broken through the surface of the medieval unity in the late Middle Ages in the struggle around Occamism and which began its visible course with the Renaissance, was accompanied by the rise of radically different philosophies or "words." It is legitimate to say that this dissolution was caused by the rise of many philosophies, that is to say, of different claims for truth. Gusdorf rightly stresses another aspect of the enigmatic role of language in man's highest aspirations in quoting in his book a letter of the young Descartes, who in modern thinking constitutes the principal watershed, to Father Mersenne in 1629 (Gusdorf, *op. cit.,* pp. 25 ff.). Descartes gives in this answer his opinion on a project for a universal language made by Mersenne, and continues by saying that the invention of such a language depends on the true philosophy (*" la vraie philosophie "*). Such inventions arise from time to time. The current universal languages (Esperanto, Volapük) are only bastards of this intention. They are made for practical purposes, but inspired by an idealism for universal brotherhood and peace which has kinship with Descartes's vision. In our time of ever-increasing complexity of knowledge and of regression of real culture, a kindred idea is behind " basic English " and " basic French." We all know of the repeated endeavors to construe language in which the significance of each word is clearly circumscribed in the hope that such a language might become the instrument of universal scientific discourse without any risk of misunderstanding. It is not the place here to enter into the critical questions that must be put with regard to all these endeavors, fruits of a certain type of idealist rationalism, from the standpoint of linguistics, which deals with languages as a living organism and structure.

It is, however, in the context of our subject, necessary to raise the theological question: What is behind the fervent desire of a Descartes and why does he link it so intimately to the quest for *the* only true philosophy? In the light of the Bible it is the longing back of man toward his primeval state of true normality, to the stage before the Tower of Babylon, when the whole earth was of one language. Or to put it differently: it is the desire to be again like Adam, who called every creature by its name as expression of its true nature; or to be like the Holy Spirit, who restored the universal intelligibility of language. In this Biblical perspective we clearly see the contradictory nature of man's deepest impulses: on the one hand the yearning for wholeness; on the other hand, the desire to be like God, the original sin. So the highest philosophical aspirations lie under the predicament which is expressed in the Bible in the duality of the Tower of Babel and the event of Pentecost. The philosophers do not acknowledge this existential situation, and are unaware that they dream of Paradise Regained as their own achievement, or usurp redemption as a " robbery " (Phil. 2:6). All these dreams of the one universal language, whatever their value and significance may be in certain concrete situations, are doomed to remain utopias. This is the case not just because they contradict the actual, living reality of language, as the science of linguistics knows it. The real reason is that they contradict the reality, the given condition of man, which is marked by the fundamental fact that he reaches back to wholeness, but in vain, because he is unable to achieve it by his own power.

The reality of man is contradictory, it is truth *and* lie, order and disorder. Gusdorf's remark, " The ultimate meaning of the ' word ' belongs to the spiritual order " (cf. *op. cit.*, p. 43) , is therefore perfectly true. It must be said to Descartes's honor that he did not believe it possible to construe such a universal language, which would mean perfect knowledge and perfect peace. This, a very noteworthy fact, amounts to the avowal of this great rationalist that the quest for the true philosophy, his real aim, cannot succeed. At the same time it is remarkable that Urban, the idealist philosopher, shows in his book, which in many respects is excellent, no awareness of these deeper intricacies just because he is an idealist thinker. They can be seen only if one has the courage to see the problem of language as primarily a theological problem.

After these reflections on language, the chief instrument of communication, which led us to the profundities of human existence, we must make some observations on language in its actuality, although there too we are constantly confronted with these profundities — at least, if we have eyes to see.

Language is a social function par excellence. It is something between men. It is dialogue and therefore plays an indispensable role in communication. Language exists for communication. When we observe the development of a child, we state that the gradual mastery of speech grows out of community and through community. The quest for the origin of language, so hotly pursued by the experts, is as vain as the quest for the origin of religion. Both language and religion are always there, even in the remotest past. There are mute individuals, and there are a-religious individuals, but there are no mute communities nor a-religious communities. To be mute or a-religious is an anomaly, a deviation because language and religion are inherent in the human structure.

But would it not be more prudent not to say: Language exists for communication, but: Language ought to exist for communication? Indeed, even a superficial observation of the function of language as a social fact recommends this prudence. In fact, language serves us as much to conceal as to express ourselves. A cynic like Talleyrand used language as a means to conceal his intentions. As Mehl's fine phenomenological analysis shows (cf. his *La Rencontre de l'autrui*), communication often has the character of a combat and not of a spontaneous meeting of minds. Expression in communication needs the other, and yet can destroy the other. The art of listening is as important a part of real communication as the dialogue, as speaking. Mehl calls it " being at the disposal of the other." Why is it that true listening is a faculty of only the few? And why is it that so often so-called dialogues of thinkers are but a collection of monologues with closed ears and hearts? Is it not that man, in general, is a contradictory mixture of self-assertion and self-abandonment?

All these obvious observations, which could be endlessly multiplied, testify to the imperfection, to the problematic character of language or speech as a means of expression. Man, the perennial problem, is always implied in this whole process. The mystics, who practice the way of the flight of the alone to the Alone, have therefore always exalted " *sigē*," absence of speech, as the highest form of communication. In this contention is a weighty grain of truth, but when taken in its absolute exclusiveness it is a disastrous deviation because it is the denial of the basic significance of community in the human structure.

Many more observations could be made regarding the

dual character of language in communication and on the many metamorphoses of communication. The act of communication can mean, as already has been said, a combat, an effort to defeat each other, to prove that one is in the right; or it can mean a recognition of the other, in which case there is a real I-Thou encounter. It is, in short, an extremely complex affair.

This complexity becomes still more conspicuous when we take into consideration communication not only between individuals but between socially and culturally different groups. This demonstrates itself again in the use of language. The various languages are means of expression for different nations and peoples with a peculiar history and psychology, and a response to life which is characteristic of its special type. This is reflected in the language. In a very strong sense this holds true for the cultural differences, because distinct cultures are distinct attitudes toward life. Karl Jaspers wrote years ago his *Psychologie der Weltanschauungen* to make this point of the deep divergence in spirituality and orientation of different cultures. Cultural or social disunity, or even difference, make it very difficult to find a common language which is understandable to both sides. For communication, it is essential to understand the language of the other, and, what is more, to learn to use it. In a place like the Ecumenical Institute at Bossey, Switzerland, we had in the eight years of our directorate ample opportunity to experience this chameleonic character of language, and the barriers it poses to real communication. At Bossey this was felt more deeply because the only form of communication adequate to the ecumenical issue is not debate or discussion but the full recognition of each other. Communication, in the ideal sense of the word, presupposes a *common* universe of discourse, based on the same presuppositions and assumptions, and on the same imponderable, but very " ponderous," spontaneous reactions to the totality of life.

Here it becomes evident that translation is one of the most intricate arts. It is really appalling to one who has had much to do with languages, translation, and internationally composed meetings at which discourse must take place in different languages, to note how utterly oblivious and naïve people who know only one language are about the important subtleties involved. He who wants to get an idea of the intricate spiritual, cultural, and linguistic difficulties implied in translation should read the able books of Eugene A. Nida on Bible translation. For two reasons: The Bible is, by the nature of its case, which space forbids us to explain here, the most difficult piece of translation work in the world. In the second place, Anglo-Saxons have the ambiguous privilege of moving in one language only, whereas at the same time the Anglo-Saxon race occupies such a predominant position in the world. It is in their own interest and in that of the world as a whole that they should be especially aware of the thorny and subtle character of the problem of communication. Translation means imaginatively moving from one universe into another. If that is not possible, one speaks " different languages " in the most frustrating sense of the word.

In all that we have said about language in communication, and about translation, the two aspects of communication, which in the beginning we distinguished as " communication between " and " communication of," are represented. One should not forget, however, that, important as language is, there are many forms and means of " communication between " and " communication of " which, like language — and in certain situations even better than language or speech — create a world of meanings. It is especially necessary to emphasize this point in the area of Churches of outspoken Protestant tradition. Not without good grounds the Reformation reinstated " the Word," preaching, as one of the principal elements of the worshiping Christian community. And it will always remain necessary to maintain this point of view, because the solicitude for the proclamation and purport of the Christian message is at stake. However, from the days of the Reformation onward, this right emphasis has had such an exclusive attention that the true character of the worshiping Christian community has been seriously vitiated. Up to the present moment it has had a stifling influence on, for instance, the continuous discussions about the relation of the Word and the sacrament, resulting in the deplorable situation that the defenders of the primacy of the Word, as well as the defenders of the primacy of the sacrament, are unable to pose the whole problem of worship and evangelism with that freedom from historical and theological imprisonments which is vital to a creative and ecumenical solution.

Another consequence of this idolizing of preaching has been that in Protestant circles there is a great inhibition toward all other means of communication — as regards " communication between " and " communication of " — than speech. (A similar critique, though from a different angle, ought to be exercised on the imprisonments of the so-called Catholic tradition in the non-Roman Churches, but space does not permit this.) It is a fortunate thing that, as so often, the world forces the Church to rethink its positions. The urge for evangelism and for manifesting the apostolate of the Church, which grows mainly as a response to the illiteracy of the world in matters of the Christian religion, leads to the discovery and use of forms of communication other than speech. The Bible, notwithstanding its impressive emphasis on the Word, appears, on closer inspection, to be far more independent and free in the recognition of many forms of expression and communication as natural gifts of man, other than speech, than the Churches ever dared to be. One of my pupils, Rev. H. R. Weber, the present director of the Lay Department of the World Council of Churches, will soon publish an important report on forms of communication, which is a result of a study he made at the Graduate School for Ecumenical Studies. The title of this book, which will appear as one of the International Missionary Council Research Pamphlets, is *The Communication of the Gospel to Illiterates in Indonesia.* Among illiterates where reading and writing do not exist, one is confronted in quite a new way with the problem of the possibilities of communication. It is typical of us Westerners, who are the victims of an overwhelmingly verbal culture, that we often think that the only way to solve the problem is to make them literate first! Weber's book has become an able plea for confident experimentalism in pluriform means of communication. One could fill pages mentioning only the many efforts going on in many lands. It is also significant to mention the phenomenon of a silent revolution which is taking place in our Western world among millions of people who prefer "seeing" to "hearing" or "reading." It is significant to note that in Indo-Germanic languages the words "see" and "know" go back to the same root.

We are living in a highly rational and mechanical-technical culture. This does not mean that we, men of the present time, are in the real sense of the word "reasonable," that is to say, reasonable in regard to the deepest layers of reality. On the contrary, passionate emotionalism is a great

power. But it means that the standard approach is to conquer nature by rational analysis and technical skill. One of
the consequences is that many of the forms of communication that are given in human nature and were active in
former periods of our culture have atrophied. One of the
areas that must be reconquered is that of symbolism. Everywhere at present, in the various forms of art, in philosophy,
in science, in religion, the significance of symbolism as a
means of expression and communication is rediscovered.
Symbols are material things or representations that point
beyond themselves to a world of transcendental values and
realities. It is characteristic of our age that this rediscovery
is taking place through study. The time, the spiritual condition of the world, is not ripe for creative activity. This
" study " approach which inevitably tends toward a cerebral
perception implies the danger that it identifies symbol and
the reality to which it points. It can also degenerate in
aestheticism. Great civilizations, rich in symbolism, never
knew this degeneration because their inner urge was to express their dominant ideas, and the unintended result was
that they often were " beautiful." Yet the growing openness
for the significance of symbols as means of communication
is a hopeful sign and should be a concern of the Church,
whose message is full of symbols. Part of the difficulty of
communication of the gospel in our day is the unawareness
of the Church of the fact that the Christian message is
highly charged with symbolic connotations, and the inability of the world by the cultural situation to apprehend it.
Neither theology, nor worship, nor the forms in which worship or liturgy are expressed, nor communication of the
gospel in traditional or untraditional ways, can do without
the awareness which a grasp of symbolic " language " —
this word is taken in the sense of every possible form of

expression — creates. (Cf. *The Symposion of the Institute for Religious and Social Studies,* edited by Ernest Johnson, on "Religious Symbolism"; E. Cassirer, *Psychologie der symbolischen Formen.* It seems to me that Paul Tillich in his article on "Theology and Symbolism" in the above-mentioned symposion goes too far in his substitution of symbols for reality. He says, for instance, "It is not God that is given [which in a certain sense is true], but the symbols of the encounter between God and man" [p. 111]. Mehl rightly says that the real communication of the gospel is to transmit the presence of a "third" who is a person and not a symbol.)

It is impossible to treat in one chapter all the aspects of communication as a spiritual, social, and cultural function. Conscious of this deficiency, we want to close with some remarks on mass communication, because of its actuality and relevance to our time. An important part of the time of many people is filled by the modern technical means of information and propaganda: television, radio, and cinema. These are the media through which they obtain their "education," to use a great word for a very ambiguous thing. We cannot enter into all the implications of the media of mass communication, their pending between instrument of culture or of barbarism, the problem of "Christian" films, "Christian" radio, "Christian" television. The fundamental thing to be said is that the term "mass communication" is very ambiguous. Genuine communication is always *personal.* There are cases in which mass communication becomes personal, but in the present state of mass communication the combination of these two words "mass" and "communication" is apt to contain a misleading delusion. A great deal of what is produced by these media is propaganda, or a drugging away of the emptiness of countless people, molding the feelings and thoughts according to a pattern which makes them passive tools. Out of commercial considerations, money and inventiveness are lavishly spent. This is not the only thing that can be said about the mass media, but it should be said first, because these media have enormous demonic potentialities and realizations. They also have good potentialities. It should especially be said to and in the Church, and among Christians who with great diligence and devotion try to use these media, as it is said, for the witness to the gospel. In all these diligent efforts there is often a dangerous optimism, which regards communication as a quantitive proposition, forgetting that the crucial point is not to use them, but to *change* them. What we need is not a rejection of these media, which merely will be continuously perfected, but a critical use of them, a building up of our own criteria and style and a struggle with their demonic, culture-destroying tendencies. The Church owes as one of its services to the world, to this sector of modern life, the producing of men and women who find ways of being the conscience of the world.

# 4 *The Breakdown of Communication*

THE FACT OF THE BREAKDOWN OF COMMUNICATION, OR THE feeling that it exists, is the main cause of the intense discussion developing among Christians on the problem of communication. One must fall ill in order to reflect on what health is for life. Hence Rosenstock-Huessy rightly stresses the remarkable fact that sociology, the effort at scientific analysis and understanding of society, of community life and human relationships, was begun by Comte, Fournier, and others a hundred and twenty-five years ago at the time when the disintegration of society by the aftermath of the French Revolution, " *la grande Révolution,*" and by the industrial revolution became felt. In our third chapter we said: " Communication, in the ideal sense of the word, presupposes a *common* universe of discourse, based on the same presuppositions and assumptions, and on the same imponderable, but very ' ponderous,' spontaneous reactions to the totality of life." In this sentence the problem of the breakdown of communication as one of the great facts of our time finds its fundamental explanation. It will take us some time to see the implications, and in our discussion we shall, of course, concentrate on the breakdown of communication of the Christian message and what that means.

Before doing this, we again have to make a preliminary

remark. Those who take part, the world over, in the discussion on the breakdown or crisis of Christian communication to the world often make, it seems to me, two mistakes. The first mistake is that the breakdown of communication is conceived too exclusively as an isolated event, happening between the Church and the world. It is too much left out of account that this breakdown is a phenomenon appearing in all spheres of life. Our severely disintegrated culture is characterized by an abnormal differentiation. Differentiation as such is normal, and is one of the typical symptoms of all cultures, which have left the stage of archaic civilization. But at present, in our Western world, differentiation is abnormal, a sign of illness. These signs of cultural illness are not necessarily and exclusively fatal. In many cases they may be gropings for the recovery of health, because, as world wars have proved, the capacity for recovery in the human species to a tolerable kind of life is amazing. But this does not remove the abnormality. In the field of science specialization has gone so far that even in the same faculty it occurs that people cannot " communicate " in the right sense. The experts become more and more lonely figures, and the mass of people, also among the so-called intellectual class, belong more and more to the ignorant laity. Although it is contrary to the nature of science, the general attitude toward science is one of blind faith. All laudable attempts to popularize the various sciences in a responsible way cannot alter a bit this fundamental attitude, forced upon men by the progress of science. In other words, the world of science has its problem of communication.

In the field of art (the whole history of modern art with all its fashions and obstinate experiments offers testimony) we have a Babylonic confusion of " schools " and " tendencies," mostly blind and deaf to each other, without communication or the desire for it. The representatives of art do not express, in different ways, one common spiritual world, because there is no " one world." In other words, the world of art has its problem of communication. In the field of *Weltanschauung* (world view) — to put it as generally as possible — we have a blatant disharmony. If one only reflects on the mass of stuff, poured out daily on people by radio and film, from which every trace of unity of orientation and direction is absent, one realizes the spiritual atomization of our present world. Unity cannot be there, because the unity of culture is broken. Man in the mass (which is not the same as a mass man) lives in a world with a firmament in which the great stars fulfill their function; but he is a prey to conflicting myths. This state of things undermines the possibility of real communication.

In other words, the world of *Weltanschauung*, by this loss of communication which is also bred by the monstrous degree of urbanization we go through, is invaded by loneliness, which is in vain covered up by the hectic activity of pleasure industry. To a high degree, it is true to say that man is flying for himself and for his neighbor. He is nowhere.

The second mistake regards a point on which we have touched briefly in our third chapter, in a different context. In the feverish search for the solution of the problem of communication, a search issuing from a genuine apostolic consciousness and missionary zeal, it looks often as if it is wholly a matter of different, new language, better adapted and attuned to that mysterious elusive being: modern man. It goes without saying that this is a very important aspect, were it only for the reason that, as we demonstrated, language and communication are intimately related, but it should be stressed that to the breakdown of communication the greatest contributor is the social and spiritual crisis of today. We shall come back to it. Yet it is only possible to get a full grasp of the problem of communication if we see that it cannot simply be mended by a different language, or theology, whether called " experimental " or " radically revised," important as these are. Rather, it is inherent in the cultural predicament and social revolution, in which we simply find ourselves as a life pattern, that there is, and cannot but be, a problem of communication. Just as in politics we are seeking, according to Molotov's word in Geneva, " for the same language," we are doing this too in the area of culture.

What are the causes of the breakdown of communication, especially in regard to the Christian message and the function of the Church in the world? A note of warning has to be given here. The above analysis is, inevitably, written from a European background. We are fully aware of the fact that the scene of America and even that of Great Britain often has very different emphases and colors when compared with Continental Europe. Yet it is our conviction that what we try to say holds true for the five continents of the world. Professor Urban stresses in an eloquent way, in his book *Language and Reality,* the necessity of a common universe of discourse for communication, for communication in itself, even if adequate, does not *create* " community "; it *presupposes* community. So we could state the problem in the terms that there is a lack of community, and it is true that one of the outstanding marks of our age is a longing for real community, which constitutes true cohesion and participation of the same apperception of the value and purpose of life. With this key word " community " it is easy to seize immediately on the key problem of the Church, which by its nature and divine purpose should be the embodiment of true community, as we know by the central place of *koinōnia* in the New Testament as one of the new facts in Jesus Christ. For the moment, however, we do not pursue this line. When speaking about causes of the breakdown, after all, the best way is to compress it in the word "secularization," in spite of the fact that it is used in season and out of season, and so in danger of becoming meaningless.

What is secularization? Is it, from the point of view of the Church, only the great enemy which we must incessantly try to strangle, and then we are safe again? In many cases the diatribes of Christian orators give this impression. This is a fatal blunder, which is made worse by the fact that people speak as if this wicked demon, secularization, is only a trait of the world, outside ourselves, not present in us, Christians, nor in the Church. This fatal blunder is ubiquitous, committed in all so-called Christian countries, but it seems that the Anglo-Saxon world is in a special danger to fall victim to it. We think about Great Britain, where the Christian tradition seems still to maintain some pervasive power, which on the European continent with its revolutionary convulsions is destroyed. Or about America, where the advance of religion and of increasing Church membership, stands in intriguing contrast to the ongoing process of unchurching, happening in Europe. The truth is that everywhere the Church is thoroughly secularized, just as much as the world, although in a different way. The Church's secularization is even more serious than the world's, because one is largely blinded to it by the "holy" or "sacral" cloak in which everything is disguised.

Our personal answer to the question whether secularization has to be seen *solely* as the great enemy is no. It is the common reality of both Church and world, the historical situation in which we are placed, fraught with the greatest dangers and possibilities for human life. In such a situation of great trial it depends on how we think and act whether this trial means death or life.

Is secularization exclusively a negative post on the balance of modern life, or has it also positive aspects, especially from the Christian point of view? Our personal answer to this question is yes. There are also positive aspects, real gains. Secularization signifies undoubtedly a process of enormous spiritual slimming, a catastrophic disorientation and blindness for the normative fundamentals of life, as seen in the light of the Biblical message, but particularly among Christians it should be said that it has also a function of purification, of forcing us to a radical realism, if we are wise enough to discern and seize it. Even one should say that it contains a deserved and necessary rebuke to the Church and Christendom. In the perspective of history the Church as an official established institution has been, by its attitudes, unwillingly one of the greatest negative causes of the triumphant rise of secularism in the sense of man's taking his destiny wholly in his own hands. It is sometimes helpful to remind oneself of the original use of the word "secular." It stems from the Middle Ages, which tried to master the life of society by the famous distinction between the temporal or secular order and the spiritual or sacral order, the last having the primate. In canonical law it meant civil society. The secular clergy was, and is, the clergy not belonging to a monastic order, and therefore, although of the Church, also belonging to the "saeculum," the temporal order, as distinct from the renunciation of the world incorporated in the monastic orders as representing the perfect Christian way of life. Secularization originally meant the expropriation of the Church, of lands, possessions, rights and privileges, by the State. These political acts of secularization were as well a sign of the breakdown of the medieval system as a manifestation of the gradual emancipation of society and the individual from the established authority of the Church — a new form of the famous medieval struggle between pope and emperor, or Church and State, but this time the State having the best cards in its hand in the interplay of power.

Secularization as a revolutionary spiritual and cultural event, we always date from the Renaissance. The signum of our present time is that we are, in our present "worldly" or "secular" orientation, drawing the last consequences of this age-long struggle which started as a movement for liberation, in the name of the dignity of man and the endless possibilities of man to unveil the mysteries of the universe and to master life. The cardinal fact at present is that this whole irrepressible movement of absolute self-sufficient self-reliance has resulted on the one hand in a rational and technical mastery of nature, which revolutionizes our whole look and attitude toward life, and on the other hand in the pandemonium of a Babylon as never witnessed in history, leading us into enslavements to self-invented myths and illusions, which undermine the very basis of decent human existence. Both elements remain inextricably mixed, liberation and enslavement.

One of the causes of closedness to the Church and its message, especially in the world of intellectuals, is that somehow the inimical negative attitude, taken in the past on the whole by the Church to this dominant tendency, remains indelibly imprinted on the minds of people. By and large, in many respects the ambiguous and great achievement of the modern way of life has been a conquest on a recalcitrant Church. The historical necessity of the movement for a man-made world is proved by the fact that also in the nineteenth and twentieth centuries it has followed its relentless course, and the Church, in spite of many revivals of great significance, has never been able to stop it and took only a defensive attitude. A real Christian answer has still to be given, and the search for such an answer is the great task ahead of the Church.

Another aspect of the secularization is symbolized in the expropriation of the Church by the State to which we referred above. Was it legitimate or illegitimate usurpation of the State to do so? Juridically speaking, many questions could be raised here, but this is entirely outside our concern. What concerns us is that in this political procedure just as in the cultural declaration of independence from ecclesiastical guardianship, there was hidden a deserved rebuke of the Church's usurpation of worldly power and acquisition, and of its cramping authority over the intellectual and moral responsibility of man. The secularization of the world revealed the secularization, that is to say, the world conformity, of the Church in the period when it proclaimed and asserted the supremacy of the sacral over the secular, by conforming to the motives and methods of the world, which is in essence apostasy from its true nature and calling. This is one of the aspects of what we call the function of purification, contained in secularization. To put it in a different way, the whole process of secularization is one of the ironic ways of God to call the Church back to its true nature and calling, to knowing better its legitimate pretension to proclaim and assert Christ's claims of Kingship over all realms of life, but to do this, just as its Lord, as a servant, even ready to be a suffering servant, and not as a power dependent on rights and privileges. It is a call back to Rom. 12:1, 2: " I beseech you therefore, brethren, by the mercies of God, that ye present your bodies a living sacrifice, holy, acceptable unto God, which is your reasonable service. And be not conformed [*syschēmatizesthe*] to this world: but be ye transformed [*metamorphousthe*] by the renewing of your mind, that ye may prove what is that good, and acceptable, and perfect will of God." In this verse the *Biblical* " canonical law," so to speak, is contained. It is my sincere conviction that the Church will do one of the most effective acts in overcoming the lamented breakdown of communication, if it hears this call of God as it comes to it through the similarly lamented phenomenon of secularization. That would be something quite different from its hesitant, complaining, defensive attitude, which is hitherto mainly the case. Has the Church really heard this divine voice toward self-examination and self-correction in the cloak of secularism? Adequately? It seems not. Far and wide the Churches are in one sense or another, whether officially or not, " established " bodies, and lack the courage and the faith to see that a serious handling of this state of affairs, *as a problem of the first spiritual magnitude,* is a far more effective answer to the breakdown of communication than the best-organized evangelistic campaigns.

Another aspect of this function of purification in secularism is, from the Christian point of view, the fact that it is now easier than in the days when the authority of Christian tradition was still strong to see more clearly the right border lines between Church and world. It is now easier to understand that the real Church is always a minority, and therefore should be neither elated by rapidly increasing nor distressed by rapidly decreasing membership, but take both as a signal, calling it to discover God's and the devil's purpose in it. Do we see? Do we understand? Have we real discernment to " prove what is that good, and acceptable, and

perfect will of God "? If so, we are paying a substantial con-
tribution to the overcoming of the breakdown of communication. If not so, we must accept the fact that we continue
in brilliantly analyzing the problem, without power, because our minds are not really " transformed." Therefore,
such a radical new conception of the Church's position in
the midst of the world is not a retreat, but a reseizure of its
authentic nature, and consequently dynamic.

Secularization is, next to the great upsurge of autono-
mous thinking with all its beneficial and disastrous results,
also caused by the great shattering of age-old life patterns
by the industrial and technical revolution, and what followed in its wake. The world has totally changed. Urbanization, with its enormous conglomeration of people, atom-
ized in their relationships, not only has destroyed well-knit
community life all over the world, but has as its inherent
tendency that it hampers the building-up of stable community life. One of the automatic results of this dynamic social revolution is that the Church as an influential factor
has faded out of the lives of millions.

The changed world in which the Church lives and of
which it is a part requires not only a rethought theology,
an intelligent grasp of the cultural situation, but a thorough awareness of the radically changed sociological factors, and the sociological conditionedness of cultural and
religious life patterns, in and outside the Church. Middle
classes of a new type, with a different kind of bourgeois
mentality, are the result of the industrial revolution. No
less evident is the amount of dislocation and mobility in all
classes, accompanied by a spiritual nomadism or paralysis,
which baffles everybody who is concerned about the communication of the Christian message.

This social revolution, the new role of the state and of

civil government as providers of social security and even
of colossal service organizations for mending social and
moral (!) ills — developments which lie in the logic of social progress — means for the Church a great *loss of function,* caused by the changed conditions and by the inadapt-
ability of the Church. At the same time it means a growing
dominance of humanitarian thinking in the conduct of
these new patterns, which, although it has originally its
roots in Christian notions, alienates imperceptibly the
minds of great masses from the Christian faith, which is at
best regarded as the particular concern of Churches, without universal relevance. Christianity is in the general opinion the interest of a coterie.

Moreover, the negative way in which the Church as a
whole has reacted for a long time to the industrial and social revolution, blind to their significance, and identifying
itself with the established social order, has resulted in a
great *loss of prestige* of the Church.

The enumerated facts are all well known, but it has to
be stressed that they have contributed greatly to the alienation of whole classes of people from the Christian message,
which is another way of saying: breakdown of communication. With reasons or without reasons, there is a deep-seated
conviction that the gospel and the Church are utterly
irrelevant.

We have offered this brief cultural and sociological ex-
posé in order to make clear that the breakdown of communication has superpersonal objective causes, which continuously function. It is impossible to open a direct attack on
them. We are ourselves, the Churches included, subject to
these same forces. It is important to be aware of this situation because it is a necessary help to liberate the Churches
of a very common delusion, that is to say, the delusion, pres-

ent in many Christians and Churches, to treat secularism in its widest sense as something outside the Church. Churches and Christians are to a high degree secularized. This is the case not alone in the sense which is valid for all ages, including the so-called ages of faith and of the *Corpus Christianum*, that worldly motives and sins are evident in the Church and in the lives of Christians. The Churches also are secularized in the new sense that secularized interpretations of the gospel often have the upper hand over the critical function of Biblical faith. The minds of Christians are secularized, dominated by the current principles of thinking and action. This state of affairs is particularly evident in the prevalent opinion that religious faith is an ethical opinion, that religion and ethics are identical. The central tenets of the Christian faith are ultimately irrelevant, relics of the past. The essential thing is to be men of good will, and religion is a useful thing to achieve this end. Therefore, the breakdown of communication is not only a matter between the Church and the unchurched, ignorant, indifferent masses, but is present *within* the Church between the man in the pulpit — granted the case that he really preaches Christ in his fullness — and the man in the pew. There is, of course, a different form of breakdown of communication *within* the Church, namely, the case that the man in the pew either gets a message, which is in fact a distortion of the Christian faith by its too facile accommodation to fashionable notions, or a correct doctrinal deliverance, which is stones instead of bread for those hearers who sincerely long for a relevant Christian answer to their problems and conflicts in actual life.

In an analysis of the causes of the breakdown of communication, some points require special mention because they often occur in discussions on the subject. In the first place there is the loss of authority of the Bible. Many generations have lived with the explicit or implicit belief in the infallibility of the Word of God. This has been the unassailable basis for the truth of the Christian message, to such an extent that the conviction is universal, even among those who recognize no loyalty to the Church and the gospel, that the Christian faith stands and falls with the literal infallibility of the Bible. This being so, it is natural that the vehement shock this belief suffered as a result of modern scientific Biblical research is still operative. The Christian faith, in the opinion of many, stood and stands as it were exposed as untrustworthy. The time of its undisputed authority belonged and belongs irrevocably to the past. To say this amounts to the same thing as saying that in principle the time of the *Corpus Christianum* belongs to the irrevocable past, and, let us add, should remain so. The Christian faith, if it manifests itself in its true nature, is not the message about an infallible book. It is the message about a person who " is set for the fall and the rising again of many . . . and for a sign which shall be spoken against " (Luke 2:34). (Simeon speaks here, as we know, about Israel, but his statement applies to the whole world, the so-called Christian world included. Therefore, we have dropped the words " in Israel " from the quotation.) In the spiritual and cultural sphere, however, this blow to the ancient doctrine about the infallible Bible has had a disastrous influence on both believers and unbelievers. To the Protestant wing of Christendom, for a long time this doctrine afforded a security similar in kind to the doctrine of the infallible Church held by the Catholic wing. There are significant differences, but it is not our duty to expand on them. The steady march of Biblical research has, in many respects, shattered this security, this last refuge against doubt and anxiety. It has also given

weapons to many people, who are called " freethinkers," to
combat Christianity by exposing the ridiculousness of the
Bible, using and abusing the results of research in the Bible
as an important literary fact. The upshot of this whole process, which is still going on, is that the Bible, which since the
rise of Bible societies has become the most printed and dis-
tributed book in the world, has also become to numberless
people, both Church members and unchurched, a closed
book. One might even say, a sealed book. The importance
of this fact cannot easily be overestimated in regard to the
whole problem of the breakdown of communication, because the indispensable, inspirational Source Book No. 1
of faithful communication is the Bible and nothing else.
There are various reasons for the Bible's having become in
many respects a closed and sealed book. There is a wide-
spread feeling that reading the Bible cannot anyhow be a
profitable affair. This feeling is still an effect lingering from
the original shock to the belief in its infallible authority.
There is particularly among the majority of lay members
of the Church a feeling of helplessness in regard to the
Bible. They, of course, have a vague attitude of reverence
for the Book, but don't know what to do with it. It sounds
so strange, so incomprehensible, so distant from their ordinary ways of thinking. It is, at best, to them a " sacral " language, as all sacral languages wrapped up in mystery. It is,
they think, a book for experts and theologians.

This brings us to a very vital point in the whole question
of communication and its breakdown; and at this point,
again, hosts of Church people and entirely unchurched people go arm in arm. We must recognize the unintelligibility
of the Bible, not only of its language, its terminology, but
also, to use a German word, of its *Weltbild* (picture of the
world) . This affects people as antiquated, archaic, unscien-

tific. Especially, this last impression is devastating, or at least embarrassing, because it belongs to the lifeblood of modern man that being "scientific" is the arbiter and guarantee of truth and nothing else. Our skeptical, unbelieving, but very polytheistic age has science as one of its high gods.

We touch here upon a fundamental point regarding the breakdown of communication. It is unnecessary to tabulate the subjects which interest people in our rationalized and technicized world, with the atom bomb as its crowning top, in order to prove the thesis that this thoroughly immanent, but undoubtedly very productive, way of thinking and reacting to the totality of the world seems entirely unconnected with the concerns of the Bible. The great Biblical key ideas of sovereign divine creation, of covenant, election, sin, mercy, judgment, conversion, rebirth, reconciliation, justification, sanctification, Kingdom of God, are utterly alien, and consequently irrelevant, to people whose minds are molded and dominated by the conquest of the kingdom of man. They are undecipherable hieroglyphs, with which, strangely enough, Church people still seem to play. I am fully conscious that this picture is somewhat overdrawn, because I am not ignorant of the fact that great writers and artists, also a handful of thinkers, who own no allegiance to a Church, in their central myths, symbols, and speculations manifest a remarkable awareness of spiritual realities, which hovers around some Biblical key ideas. But it cannot be my object to give a complete picture of the complex spiritual and cultural situation of our time. The decisive point in connection with the breakdown of communication is the dominant trend in the modern apperception of the totality of life, which seems to be worlds apart from the Biblical apperception. The last is Chinese to the ordinary man. There is an incompatibility of languages to the extent, it seems, of mutual intranslatability. It seems an insoluble dilemma.

The well-known controversy around the theology of R. Bultmann, expressed in the ugly word "*Entmythologisierung*" (demythologizing), has to be seen against this background. Due recognition must be given to the fact that here we have one of the greatest New Testament scholars, one of the ablest Biblical interpreters, who is so concerned, perhaps it is better to say so obsessed, with this dilemma of the incompatibility of the Biblical and the modern forms of interest and concern that he attempts to force a solution. by discarding what he considers the archaic mythological and unacceptable *Weltbild* of the Bible in this age of electricity — to use his own words — and proposing a radical " demythologizing " of the Christian message. One should not forget that Bultmann's impelling motive is not a rationalistic destruction of the Biblical message in the name of science. On the contrary, it is missionary. He intends, in doing so, to transmit in a relevant and, to the modern mind, comprehensible way the " essence " of the gospel. Time forbids us to entertain a full discussion of Bultmann's theology, which according to some observers — I doubt whether they are right — puts Barth's theology in the shadow. The whole modern debate around myth, reason, revelation, the so-called adult (*mündig*) thinking of science and their relation to each other, the problems implied in the *Weltbild* issue, the questions of form and content, would have to be reviewed and evaluated. (Books that are in many respects helpful reading are: E. Buesz, *Geschichte des mythischen Erkennens;* G. Gusdorf, *Mythe et métaphysique*.)

Therefore we are forced to compress our evaluation in

some sentences which sound dogmatic but are not meant as such. In our opinion the greatest value of Bultmann's position is that he has put in a very blunt way a cardinal question, with which the theologians by no means have dealt adequately. This being granted, it seems to me that the significance of Bultmann's attempt is vastly overrated, especially in Germany. He labors with an antiquated conception of myth, which is unaware of what present-day scholars in the sciences of religion and of anthropology, and philosophers of great caliber have found about myth as one of the *perennial* forms of human expression and modes of human knowledge. It has been a sensation that the existentialist philosopher Karl Jaspers in a lecture given at Bâle in 1953 (published, with the discussion, in *Schweizerische Theologische Umschau,* June, 1953, under the title " Wahrheit und Unheil der Bultmannschen Entmythologisierung ") rejected Bultmann's attempt, with all due respect for his scholarly standing. Bultmann reduces the " essence " of the gospel to an existentialist form of self-estimate of man in which the Christian element is that this self-estimate takes place before the judgment seat, so to speak, of the cross. The father or patriarch of all types of the existentialist variety, Sören Kierkegaard, who in a different setting treated the scandal of God in the flesh in history, in his *Philosophische Brocken,* in a way full of profound originality, could, in my view, have cured Bultmann of his wrong way of putting the question. I fully agree with Dietrich Bonhoeffer in his *Letters and Papers from Prison* (pp. 125 and 145 ff.) where he says that Bultmann in his reductional procedure is a typical liberal theologian (i.e., dropping the so-called mythological elements of the Christian message in order to preserve its essence) and where he maintains that the mythical concepts must be maintained. This judgment of Bonhoeffer's is the more impressive because he attaches, with Bultmann, such a high value to the "adultness" (*Mündigkeit*) of the modern mind, for which, as Jaspers has rightly observed, the appearance of science as a dominant factor in his outlook is "the deep incision in human history" (*Der philosophische Glaube,* p. 153).

Returning to our starting point — the deeply disturbing effect of modern Biblical research, whether destructive or constructive — what is our final judgment of this effect in the light of our subject: the breakdown of communication? We do not hesitate, fully conscious of the anxieties, confusions, and errors to which it has led, to call it a blessing in disguise. Years ago (in 1905) one of the ablest and sincerest theologians, a minister in the Dutch Reformed Church, made a great stir when, in a sermon, he tried to explain to the frightened members of the Church the real significance of so-called higher criticism. His sermon had as its text Matt. 14:22 ff., the story about Jesus walking on the stormy sea. The disciples first cried out in fear, because they thought it was "a spirit" (*phantasma*), but then Jesus, speaking straightway to them, said: "Be of good cheer; it is I; be not afraid." This is what I mean by "blessing in disguise." The rise and growth of modern scientific research of the Bible as a fruit of the secularist urge of the modern world, in spite of its many errors and false intentions, is an instrument in God's hand to liberate the Church and the Christians out of their entrenchment in wrong positions and hiding places. It is humiliating to note, as so often, also in these cases that "the world" is the liberator of the Church. This is God's sovereign way of dealing with his people, when it evidently lives by fear, and not by faith. The Church needed this great shock, because it lived on a wrong foundation, i.e., that *the Bible* is the truth, forgetting that the Bible teaches that *Jesus Christ* is the Truth, " for other foundation can no man lay than that is laid, which is Jesus Christ " (I Cor. 3:11).

From this point of view the enormous growth of fundamentalism with its fanatic emphasis on the literal inerrancy of the Bible *as the first article of faith* is a spiritual disease. All this stress on infallibility is a crude intellectualism, a dismal religious disorientation. It would sound like a false note if we spoke about God, our Lord, the Holy Spirit, the Word of God, as infallible. It is un-Biblical. The Bible speaks about God, Christ, the Holy Spirit, the Word of God, as true and faithful. In all parts of the Christian Church, especially under that part of the Church subsumed under the name " sects," fundamentalism is a disturbing fact. It is a refusal to leave the wrong hiding place. It is in our historical juncture escapism in quasi-heroic garb. It is a refusal to face the situation in which God has placed us in this modern world, which is also under the care of his providence. By no means should these sentences be taken as all that can be said about the complex phenomenon of fundamentalism. It is also in many respects a reaction against irresponsible freethinkerlike theology in universities and pulpits, and a rebuke to the Church which has not found the way to give guidance to its members, perplexed by the theories of critical scholars, by a clear and unsophisticated interpretation of the issues involved. This escapism is not a specialty of fundamentalist sects. It is a spiritual disease, present in most Churches today. The so-called liberal view of the authority of the Bible can, in no sense, be a remedy to the disease, because it is itself, with all its good intentions, an evidence of religious debilitation.

The authority of the Bible has been shaken because it was built on a wrong basis. The wrong basis was the doctrine of its infallibility. The right understanding of this "unmasking" does not weaken, but strengthens, the authority of the Bible. Modern Biblical research, though not always by intention — and so being an unwilling instrument of God — has been an immense help in showing, more clearly than could be done by any dogmatic assertion, that the only knowledge of God, which radically breaks the spell of all naturalistic, moralistic, or mystical religion, is to be acquired through the Bible, the instrument of God's Word. The miracle of the Bible is not its infallibility, but the fact that a constant intercourse with it proves that " the word of God is quick, and powerful, and sharper than any two-edged sword, piercing even to the dividing asunder of soul and spirit, and of the joints and marrow, and is a discerner [*kritikos*] of the thoughts and intents of the heart " (Heb. 4:12) . The possibility for modern men, utterly alienated from its key concepts and language, to understand the Bible and hear the word of God in it, is as great as for men and women in the days of the *Corpus Christianum* — perhaps even greater. Therefore, in my opinion, one of the primary means of overcoming the breakdown of communication is to search, with everybody who can be persuaded to do so, the Scriptures, without any theories *about* the Bible, and so to open the way for a possible experience of Heb. 4:12, because the Bible is " a discerner . . . of the heart," which is in all ages, mentalities, and cultures the same, although it does not react always and everywhere in the same way.

The attitudes taken by Churches and their members, all over the world, in the face of the breakdown of communication are endlessly varied. Most of the Churches and their members, in spite of the stirrings for evangelism as a program, are still blind and complacent. Their introvert pro-

pensity of mind keeps them indeed unaware of the fact
that the world has radically changed, and that they con-
stitute, from the sociological angle, a club with special in-
terests, out of real contact with the world. To be sure, in
their midst these truths are mentioned and even sometimes
discussed, but it does not work like a rude shock. It does
not become the spring of new searching, vision, and action,
which leads to the necessary radical change, in the first
place, in the life itself of the Churches. One is often content
with propaganda for the Church as it is, and with a drive
for increase of membership.

There is also a deeper-going disturbance, leading to experiments in evangelism and communication, often exe-
cuted with great daring and perseverance. Our apprecia-
tion of these experiments, however, is strongly mixed with
the feeling of their inadequacy to the degrees of alienation
from the gospel and the Church — especially the last — a
feeling amounting in many cases to desperation. The well-
known French Christian leader, Jacques Ellul, one of the
most penetrating minds of the Church as a whole, speaks
for many serious Christians, passionately immersed in the
breakdown of communication, when he says, " One primary
statement of fact, which stands out clearly when we reflect
upon our Church life, and our Christian action, is *the fundamental weakness of our evangelization.*" (*The Presence
of the Kingdom,* p. 138; italics mine.)

It is only about twenty years ago that in Europe and
Great Britain some leading people, mainly from the background of the Student Christian Movement and of missions, began to raise their voices about the " missionary
situation " of the Church in Europe. They appealed to
their fellow Christians to see realistically the fact that the
Church in the so-called Christian countries finds itself prac-

tically living in a dechristianized, pagan, nihilistic world, and to draw the consequences. (It is my conviction that this applies as well to the United States of America, notwithstanding the religious floodtime there at present.) It is only since then that the serious concern about apostolate, evangelism in quite new terms, communication and its breakdown, rose steadily on the ecumenical horizon. Many of the most gifted and vocal intellectual Christians, gripped by this situation, spoke even of the " post-Christian " era, in which we are living. As a clarion call to sleeping churches and to slumbering Christians, this is a very helpful term. (Sleeping and slumbering is not synonymous with inactive. Active churches can be sleeping in regard to the essential issues, and there are many sleeping churches.) In the context of this view, the Constantine period of Christianity, which was the beginning of apostasy, had now come to an end. Constantine was considered the great criminal who started this period. Again, in a world of sleeping or drowsy churches and Christians, this way of speaking, even in strident terms, has its great value, and, what is still more, its right. When men of such caliber as the Roman Catholic Romano Guardini, who lives intensely on the frontier of Church and world, in a book called *Ende der Neuzeit* (End of the Modern Age) speaks about this whole situation in realistic and at the same time in apocalyptic tones, there is reason to stress this right. It is too much forgotten in our traditionalist rural, and our self-satisfied middle-class, churches, that an apocalyptic estimate of *every* situation belongs to the very genius of Biblical faith, and is not, if set in its right place, despondent escapism, but the realism of faith. Besides this, however, it must be said that the term " post-Christian " can also be misleading and one-sided, doing no justice to the complexity and impredictability of the cultural situation, and to the providence of God in relation to Church *and* world both, also in a secularized world.

Finally, there is the intriguing and impressive attitude of the great Christian, Dietrich Bonhoeffer. It is found in his *Letters and Papers from Prison,* and, by the nature of the circumstances, elaborated only in a sketchy way, which leaves many questions open. Time and again Bonhoeffer turns to a theme that seems to obsess him. Briefly, it is that he calls for a real *Christian* Church in a *religionless world.* How is this possible? is his problem. His presuppositions are that the modern world is religionless in principle and in fact. It is " *mündig,*" adult, and must be taken seriously as such. The core of the problem of communication is: How can we Christians, how can the Church, speak religionlessly about God, that is to say, without the relative, time-conditioned metaphysical and spiritual presuppositions of religion? We should live in the world as if there were no God, and so achieve solidarity with our religionless world, and demonstrate that religion and faith, in the light of the Christian revelation, are quite different realms. *God's* Reign, *God's* Kingdom, and its coming, are the central concern in the midst of this situation. The Church is no real Church if not eschatological, that is to say, if not constantly living in expectancy.

In reading and pondering Bonhoeffer's reflections, born in such an existential situation of being every minute under the shadow of death in a Nazi prison, one feels deeply the great loss the whole Christian Church has suffered by the, humanly speaking, premature death of such a man for whom the decisive point was not to find new *concepts* but to hear the voice of God leading to new revealing *acts* of the power of the gospel through the Church. His participation in the common search for a new embodiment of the proclamation, in words and acts, would have been invaluable. One would have got then the opportunity to question him about this " *Mündigkeit* " of modern man, and about the irreligiousness of the modern world. I for my part agree in principle with Bonhoeffer that religion and faith in the Biblical faith are fundamentally different. I agree too that if we analyze the dominant creative urges of our modern world, it is, objectively speaking, a religionless world, in the sense of living totally without God and being able to manage without him. In this questioning, however, I would feel a great need to make some critical observations on the " *Mündigkeit* " of modern man, and on the fact, that the modern world, which *should,* if it drew the consequences of its primary attitudes and affirmations, be religionless. The modern world is, in fact, the most prolific producer of new religions, cults, pseudo religions, and idolatries there ever was, demonstrating thereby that man has an ineradicable religious appetite. This would mean a radical revision of Bonhoeffer's thesis, which is nevertheless extremely valuable, because it constrains us to grapple with the great problem of the Church today.

~

Secularism, *in* the Church and *in* the world; breakdown of communication, *in* the Church and *in* the world, and between the Church and the world — we have tried in a short compass to select some cardinal aspects of this event of great portent. On the one hand it means that the world, Christians and Churches included, verges on the edge of chaos. On the other hand, in all this chaotic confusion there is something going on suggesting in an awesome way a vision of a fan in God's hand, and a purging of the floor (see Matt. 3:12) , of the possibility of a Church, *if it sees things in God's light,* that can become more honest. Under this angle, it is justified in speaking with the Dutch theologian H. Berkhof of " the blessing of secularization," provided one couples this with the fervent prayer: " Lead us not into temptation, but deliver us from evil."

# 5 *Restoring Communication*

THERE IS A FRENCH SAYING: "*Aux grands maux les grands remèdes*" ("Great evils need great remedies"). This certainly applies to the Churches in regard to the communication of the Christian message. It is, however, very important how we interpret the word "*grand*" (great) in both cases, the "*maux*" (evils) and the "*remèdes*" (remedies). At any rate, it need not necessarily mean "spectacular" as to organization or method. It should certainly mean: the courage to go quite new ways. And where should we locate the "*maux*" and the "*remèdes*"? Without doubt in both Church and world. What does the expression "communication of the Christian message" imply? Surely more than verbal transmission, new and to the point as it may be.

With such questions in the back of our mind we undertake a critical consideration of possible answers to the breakdown of communication, when taking into account the discordant and confused reality in which our world of today lives and moves.

In a previous chapter we stated the fact that by the loss of unity of culture and of common fundamental presuppositions and attitudes — *the* deep cleavage in the world since the eighteenth century — there is an appalling lack of spiritual cohesion; and today we live in a Babylonian confusion of ideas and languages. Man has taken his destiny into his own hands. He has done and does marvelous things, but the Biblical story of the Tower of Babel repeats itself. This confusion is aggravated by another fact, i.e., that by our modern means of mass communication we are producing an ever-increasing amount of confusion, although it should be noted that in the midst of this cacophonic exhibition of our spiritual disintegration new threads of intercourse and mutual discovery are also developing in a groping way. The well-known French sociologist André Siegfried has recently published a booklet, *Aspects du XXᵉ siècle* (Aspects of the Twentieth Century), in which he characterizes European society as " the age of publicity," a huge system for molding people into definite patterns, divesting them of real personality and shaping them into spiritual robots.

This one fact proves sufficiently that the answer to the breakdown of communication of the Christian message cannot be a single answer, but must be multiple.

Moreover, we should not forget that the vast masses ("masses" is not meant in the sense of the people in the street, but indicates people of all classes and grades of education and culture) existing outside the Church or on its fringes have the impression, deeply rooted in them, that particularly the world of Churches is one of Babylonian confusion. Although many of their vague notions are mistaken, their conviction is strong in this regard, and essentially they are right. Their impression is probably strengthened by the fact that the very existence of the ecumenical movement, for the time being, accentuates this Babylonian condition in the Churches, because the ecumenical movement has to expose this Babylonian confusion in order to find the way to overcome the scandal.

One of the central concerns of the World Council of

Churches is to strengthen in all Churches the spirit of evangelism, of communicating the gospel to and in the world, and to provide the Churches with trustworthy material as to the evangelistic situation all over the world. (We mention here, e.g., the "Ecumenical Studies on Evangelism," published by the former Secretariat [now Department] for Evangelism.) It reveals, besides important and sometimes fascinating experiments and flashes of insight, a state of bewilderment and signs of a Babylonian confusion as regards the problem of communication *now*. A sense of helplessness pervades all efforts and discussions. This is the reason why, in many countries and Churches, the tone of many of those who are most deeply concerned about the apostolic obligation of the Churches in all conditions and situations is often shrill and strident.

This discussion, in ecumenical circles, on communication raises many questions. Behind it is a newly born apostolic zeal, growing out of a new vision of the Church and of the shock caused by the initial discovery of the dechristianization of the world of today. This zeal and this shock operate everywhere in smaller or bigger groups, in prophetic personalities, but most of the Churches as such are still oblivious of the zeal and of the shock as well.

In this discussion there is a strong element of rejection of, and dissent with, methods of evangelization, customary in the nineteenth century and in the twentieth before the Second World War, when hardly anybody had realized that the "Older Churches" were living in a missionary situation in their own environment. The revivals, the mass meetings, the colossal work of the so-called home missions, the rise of such phenomenal movements as the Salvation Army and the like, which were *the* characteristic forms of evangelism in the nineteenth and the first part of the twentieth century, are at present discarded by the most eloquent advocates of a modern apostolate, without minimizing, of course, the importance they had in their time. In the Churches today great numbers of people are still faithful to these forms, and many set all their hopes on the revival. This last point recently became very clear in the judgment, especially in Great Britain, on the evangelistic campaigns of Billy Graham. Without critically entering into the significance, the merits and demerits of these nineteenth century evangelism patterns, we want to make two remarks. They often had spectacular results as is evidenced in the radical change of many lives, but they did *not* turn the tide of secularization and of the exodus from the Churches on the continent of Europe and in Great Britain. This is an indication that they did not really meet the modern world. They could not and cannot because they were blind to its new and complex nature, and were driven, through the love of Jesus Christ, to rescue the lost, which is such a genuine Christian concern. In the second place, with few exceptions, the Churches as organized bodies were not the prime movers in this fervent evangelistic outreach. The private initiative of groups of Christians accomplished vicariously what was the very calling of the Church. At present, to a great extent through the impulses issuing from the ecumenical movement, the Church has become central, at least in the *discussions* on the communication of the Christian message. This is, theologically speaking, a great gain. Yet everything still depends on the question whether the Churches will find *together* the right response to their newly discovered centrality and responsibility. Theological insight as such is not creative. It becomes truly creative only when it is more than theology, that is to say, if this theology is the expression of the resolute, personal participation in

the activity of God and his Kingdom. The Holy Spirit is
not necessarily the inspiring companion of right theology.
It rather seems that often he sees his way working effectively, in spite of defective theology behind evangelistic
endeavors.

Another question is this: Is it right to define the present
discussion of evangelism and communication as the search
for new ways and methods in order to transmit the gospel
in the dynamic sense of the word to a world largely alienated from the Church and Christianity? Is it the same apostolic effervescence as in nineteenth century evangelism, but
with a more realistic approach to the alienation of the
world and its causes, and to the isolation and strangeness
(*in malam partem*) of the Church in regard to the world?
Or is it all this and still something else? As far as I see,
what animates the discussion is still something else. It is
the vision that the Church as the body of Christ, as the
community of those who gather around Jesus Christ, is
God's chosen instrument of the apostolate, that the empirical churches, for the time being, remain inert and unre-
sponsive, and that therefore the Church should be appealed
to. It is the conviction that the Church in this disintegrat-
ing world must rethink its whole being, structure, and
place in and with the world; that the Church must divine
the width and the depth of what is implied in being a servant to everybody and everything, in the name of the Suffering Servant, its Lord Jesus Christ, as Luther has expressed it so magnificently: " A Christian is a free Lord in
all things, and subject to none. A Christian is a slave, in
all things serviceable, and subject to everybody." It is indeed, humanly speaking, a hazardous undertaking in our
stupendous situation to bet on bodies like the empirical
Churches which are by their institutional nature and his-

torical precedents conservative and timidly prudent. And will it be possible to find in this modern world, living in quite a different universe of discourse, driven as it seems by its inherent secular orientation toward an atrophy of religion and, therefore, blind and deaf to " the things of the Spirit of God " (I Cor. 2:14), a response to the Christian message, charged with Biblical and theological terminology which seems so antiquated and historically conditioned? In other words, is the problem of communication mainly a problem of kerygma? Is it possible to make the incomprehensible kerygma comprehensible to the modern apperception of life, to translate and vitalize it in such a way that it is at least recognized as relevant par excellence to the real needs of man and to the world, which seems to thrive so excellently without God?

Then there is the point touched upon before: Communication of the Christian message is a complex affair in the world of today. There are different levels of communication because there are different kinds of people: The ignorant, of different sorts, because one must distinguish between ignorant people in and outside the Church; the many with vague Christian reminiscences; those who are by their presuppositions and attitudes, by their *Weltanschauung,* closed to any serious interest in it; those who by their own explanation of the Christian faith have explained away its very essence in such a way that it is hardly possible to communicate with them; the followers of the many pseudo or *Ersatz* religions, which seek for an intelligent understanding of the meaning of life and want some kind of hallowing of life; the nihilists of the indifferent variety in whom all need for asking for a deeper meaning of life seems to be extinguished; and the nihilists as it were by fate, because the bottom has not so much fallen out of

their existence, but has never been there, as a result of environment and circumstances in which they were born,
were reared, and live. The list could be continued. It is clear
that this condition of affairs requires widely different ways.

Dr. H. Hoekendyk, in an article written in 1952 in the
well-known Dutch magazine *Wending,* caused a great stir
by his provocative attack on the present state of evangelism
through the Churches. One of his contentions was that the
Churches at present do not function any more except in
the cultural milieu of what he called " the third man." By
this term he meant the bourgeois world, the product of
classical and Christian culture in which the cultivation of
personality is still vaguely or consciously the normative idea.
The Church, however, he continued, does not function in
the milieu of " the fourth man," a species not yet to be met
in concrete, but nevertheless existing already as an *" Idealtypus "* in the phenomenological sense of the word. He is
the type of the future. His essential traits are: He is a con-
formist in rebellion (cf. Camus' well-known book *L'Homme
révolté*). He is the representative of the post-Christian,
post-bourgeois, post-personal, probably of the post-religious
period, which is the close of our " modern " history. The
point which Hoekendyk wants to make above all by these
sociological observations (he acknowledges his indebtedness
in this respect to the book by Alfred Weber, *Kulturge-
schichte und Kultursoziologie*) is that his " fourth man "
has no longer any stamina for personal decision, a faculty
in man to which the existing evangelism automatically appeals. He urges that this fiction of personal decision should
be dropped, and a new group method should be sought in
evangelism.

The reading of Hoekendyk's article is extremely stimulating and illuminating. It uses the insights of sociology

in a very intelligent way. The recent research of what might be called " depth sociology," which uncovers to us the dominant structures of modern society with their enormous molding and determinative power on man as a person, raises the serious question whether there will remain some space for being a true man. This appalling question alone is sufficient to show that the prediction of " the fourth man " is not merely a figment of a sociologist's brain. There are powerful trends in the development of the structure of present society which make it one of the calamitous possibilities, and a pertinent question to those concerned about evangelism and communication. It would mean an essential change in man, just as Communism is announcing its new " Soviet man " as a being essentially different from man as known up until now. The question should be put: Has the Christian faith any chance of functioning in such a world? The problem of communication takes on, in this aspect, quite new aspects. The Church should see that it is challenged in its most essential activities and affirmations by the relentless march of the *objective* technological and mechanical powers in modern society toward robotization.

Yet, although it is *wise,* it seems to me, *to count* seriously with sociological prophecy or insight as an eye opener, it is *unwise to make it a basis* of our thinking and action as Hoekendyk seems to urge. From a sociological point of view, in the light of the endless variety of social types, it is far too generalizing and, moreover, preposterous to herald one type of man. From the *theological* point of view, it contains an impermissible neglect of the reality of the Church in Christ, which remains a fact in spite of the lamentable weakness of the empirical Church, and is a cause of a never-ending possibility of renewal of the Church. The Holy Spirit is a reality which lies outside the calculations and observations of the most able sociologists. From the *human* point of view, it is an obligation of the Church and of vital forces in the world to vindicate the true nature of the Church, not in order to save " the third man " but in order to save man.

It is significant, however, that the " radar type " of man, as described by Riesman in *The Lonely Crowd,* has much similarity with the " *Idealtypus* " of " the fourth man " of Weber, and shows that evangelism and communication have to take them into account. We must beware of the fallacy that in the past, in the so-called age of faith, of the *Corpus Christianum,* communication of the Christian message was not a problem. Consciously it was not, because the kerygma was practically the universally accepted ideology. In fact it was, because this doubtless assent was in many cases the brake on real communication. These observations add a new aspect to the complexity of the problem of communication.

After all that has been said, we can summarize the situation in the following way. The Church today lives in a secularized and disintegrated mass society, which is unusually dynamic. It behaves, however, in many respects, as if it still lived in the old stable and parochial world. In the past, and in many respects in the present too, the Church was quite naturally identified with the dominant social structure. The dynamic pace of social change has, to a certain extent, altered this, but the real blessing disguised in this revolution, that is to say, that the Church gets to learn the lesson that nonidentification with any social structure belongs to its true nature, has still to be discovered. This does not mean that the Churches have not at all tried to adapt themselves to the mobile structure of modern society. To a certain extent they undoubtedly have, but in many cases blindly, in self-defense. Their style, their atmosphere, their mode of respectability are, however, essentially unchanged. They reflect past historical stages in which the types who are alienated from Church and Christianity would not feel at home, even if they became converted. Hence, in the debate about evangelism and communication we hear the constantly recurring cry for a reform of structure, or for para-parochial congregations. Therefore one of the guiding motives behind the once-famed movement of the "worker priests" in France was to live in radical solidarity with modern laborers, apart from any parish connection. These facets are all implied in the problem of the communication of the Christian message.

The only conclusion to be drawn from all these reflections — they could easily be multiplied — is that, *objectively* speaking, the Church as an institution, as a body of witness, worship, and life, is in the melting pot! *Subjectively* speaking, it is far behind this objective situation. In various cases it is prepared to adapt itself somehow, but this is quite a different thing from looking the situation of being in the melting pot straight in the face. A certain readiness for adaptation under the pressure of the changing world is perhaps an unconscious but hesitant moving in that direction. In this light, it can be said that the Churches are confronted with the question whether ultimately they act *for the sake of tactics or for the sake of faith*. This is a crucial question, a spiritual problem of the first magnitude.

Why? Because in every respect the Church — again, when looking at the objective situation — is in an unprecedented situation. For centuries the Church has lived on the sustaining power of its historical continuity and prestige. At present it is, in principle, shorn of this "advantage," if one may use this word with great critical reservations. I myself count this one of the unintended blessings of secularization, including the fact that the Church in many of its historical dominions is more and more decreasing into a minority. If the Church sees this and seizes it in the realism of faith, that is to say, with a robust trust in the power of the Holy Spirit, it will discover the sustaining power of continuity and prestige as being merely crutches, and will be glad to stride forth in faith, in the power of the forces inherent in its nature and calling. Then, I am absolutely convinced, new powers, undreamed of, creative imagination, outside of the possibilities of purely human imagination, new ways of communication transcending what can be seen by a profound cultural and social analysis of the modern world, will be released and discovered. In every respect, in regard to the world, in regard to itself and to the ecumenical movement, that great fact of modern Church history, the Church is invited into an Abrahamitic adventure, that is to say, to go forth in faith to an unknown destiny. Here lies the deep difference with living fundamentally by tactics, which in itself is a respectable thing. But living by tactics means to remain, in spite of all intelligent adaptation, well established in its place, trying to make inroads into the world, but not wandering in faith, unprotected, consciously and joyfully, to unknown goals.

These considerations may seem farfetched to many, especially in relation to the issue of evangelism and communication of the Christian message. In my opinion, they are fundamental and are therefore indispensable to the closing part of our observations on the problem of communication, always keeping in mind all that has been said in the first chapter on "communication in Biblical perspective."

I propose to summarize my remarks concerning possible

answers to the breakdown of communication under two
headings, emphasizing that in this summary there will be
no attempt to formulate all possible answers. Some possible
answers which to me seem of cardinal importance will be
given. The two headings are: the indirect way and the direct ways, both of at least equal importance, although I
should add that the indirect way is the indispensable pre-
condition of the direct ways. The indirect way begins with
the Church, not with the world. Recalling to our mind
everything said — very incompletely — about the causes of
the breakdown of communication, lying in the Church itself and in the radically changed world, my first thesis
would be: The problem of communication is not to be
solved by evangelistic activity or by building a theology of
evangelism. Both are very necessary. If one prefers, I am
prepared to say that they are a matter of life and death.
They should happen, in season and out of season. They
will, however, remain adventurous, fascinating exploits,
which will certainly yield results, even in the world of today, largely impenetrable to the " strange " message of the
Bible, but nothing more, *if the Church itself with all its empirical triviality and dignity does not radically change, in-
flamed by the desire to conform itself to its true nature as
quoted earlier from Rom. 12:2,* and so become transformed.
Dr. Hoekendyk has rightly brought into the discussion on
missions, evangelism, and communication the triad: *kērygma* (preaching), *diakonia* (service), *koinōnia* (fellowship) as the essential marks of the Church. This implies
that in the problem of communication and evangelism not
only the right *kērygma,* but *diakonia* and *koinōnia* require new manifestations. The Church should not live in
a mood of embittered or hilarious world conquest. This is
entirely against the Spirit of Him who said shortly before

he went to the cross of self-surrender, " I have overcome the world." *It should be what it is,* according to its essential nature, and that is to *be,* in all humility and imperfection, the foreshadowing of the true community of men, the embodiment of *diakonia* for Christ's sake to everybody and everything, and so to proclaim the message of God's *philanthrōpia* (love of men) with new power; because in all these three manifestations of *kērygma, diakonia,* and *koinōnia,* the essential nature of the Church is apostolic, because the Church is " sent " (John 20:21), as the Father has " sent " Jesus.

It is an uncontradictable fact that the Church (es), whatsoever valuable and great it may still represent, does not affect the world, nor even its own members as being a true community of disinterested service. At the moment of writing we commemorate the death of Sören Kierkegaard. He, who was one of the most powerful and original witnesses to the depth of the Christian faith, was in his day disturbed about Christendom to the verge of despair. This disturbance is still valid. The Church lives, to a great extent, according to " worldly " principles and standards, in contradiction with the apostolic injunction: " Be not conformed to this world." To this world also belong our imprisonment in self-glorification, pride of our past, of our prestige, of our confessions and traditions, of our new ideas of success and efficiency, of the easy moralistic, utilitarian abuse of faith as a sales article. In fact, the Church, as it empirically is, hides its true nature and therefore deservedly is considered in the modern world as one of the many so-called religious societies with a venerable, but also a very dubious, past. Therefore, the logical beginning of all efforts to overcome the breakdown of communication is a sincere self-criticism and self-purge by the Church of its historical and cultural lags and its subserviency to the dominant thought complexes of today, in the light of its divine nature and calling, because always " judgment must begin at the house of God " (I Peter 4:17). Only in this way the new self-discovery will become a dynamic power " healing the nations," and leading us into a more adequate evangelism and communication of the Christian message. Without this, all our endeavors in the field of evangelism and communication, *which must happen with all might* out of sheer joyful obedience, will somehow remain inhibited, and the many new experiments going on will remain colonizations *" extra muros."*

Will this mean that all problems will be solved in meeting this complex world, and that we will gloriously march on? Not at all. It means that there is then in this desolate, self-centered, frightened world a Church, which is a tangible witness by its being, speaking and acting to the reality of Jesus Christ, and that is enough. The rest can be left to God and to the truth of his Word: " Seek ye *first* the kingdom of God, and his righteousness; and *all* these things shall be *added unto* you " (Matt. 6:33).

So much about the indirect way, which is an endless task and a perpetual revolution. (The word " revolution " should not be taken in the ordinary political and social sense, but as preparedness to be a Church continuously " ready to listen to Christ.") The direct ways about which I propose to say something are the *methods of evangelism.* We have repeatedly stressed the point that there are many types of mentality and atmosphere. The point where the spirits diverge, often violently, is about the value of the particular method of communication and evangelism *as to its adequacy to meet what is called the modern mind,* which presupposes in itself already a specific interpretation of this

stantial theology, because it has to convey a message, which revolves around cardinal concepts on God, man, life. This is the Church's commission. It cannot say what it likes, but what is entrusted to it by God's revelation in Christ, and has to witness to the new order of life in Christ as the crisis of all actual and possible orders of life. This having been stated, we have, however, to face the fact that neither the Church nor its members are obliged to do this in a language which is accessible only to a few select, and which is in many respects antiquated, alien to people who constantly move in quite different patterns of thought and expression, many members of the Church included. The audience also has its rights. They should be enabled to *hear* the message.

Within the Churches we are still so bound by our own technical, spiritual languages that, e.g., in the case of ecumenical declarations, we are inevitably more occupied with the necessity of having a statement that can satisfy as many as possible of *us* than we are of having a common apostolic urge that can raise us to the level of producing language that can be more universally apprehended. A striking example of these perplexities was the Evanston message on the Christian hope. It is, I believe, fair to say that there was a mood of dissatisfaction about it in Evanston. This was quite natural, because the subject itself, " hope," has a universal appeal in the world of today. As to my personal opinion, it would have been quite possible to talk about eschatology (that bogey feared by so many) quite plainly as a universal human concern, and so witness to the Kingdom of God and the predicament of the world. That would have been possible, however, only if we, in the ecumenical multilogue, had made more progress in freedom from our imprisonments in our peculiar thought patterns, and in openness to the Biblical message.

In the field of communication and evangelism, we are everywhere confronted by the necessity of translation and transposition. One can either make a few fundamental remarks or write a big book on this point. My few remarks would be, first, that this translatory activity in our present situation is of an endless variety, because the mentality, speech and thought patterns of the endless variety of groups, with which communication is entered upon, must show us the way. Secondly, it requires great imagination and flexibility of spirit, in which the experience of missions and of Bible translation is illuminating. The use of apologetics in the encounter between Church and world has its legitimate place here. Barth has rejected it. Brunner defends it, calling it " eristics." It seems to me that we need apologetics badly. It depends only on the question: How? Paul Tillich is quite right in dividing theology into kerygmatic theology and apologetic theology (i.e., in encounter and discourse with the world and its thinking). Thirdly, all translation and transposition of the Christian message presupposes a genuine listening to the "neighbor" (not the opponent). It must remain an *expression* of the real import of the message. Flexibility, therefore, must have as its partner a thorough grasp of the Christian message, not primarily intellectually but by commitment. One of its secrets is directness. Here lies one of the strong points of evangelism in *profane* places. If, for example one listens to Billy Graham, one cannot but come to the conclusion that hosts of ministers preach far better in every respect. Yet he draws many people who would never come to Church or be touched by the better sermons of the ministers, but they *do* come to the salesman of religion. One of the reasons is his directness, which is in the Church always paralyzed by pulpit, dress, stateliness, etc. Fourthly, language, communication, in our present secularized world, with all its spiritual and social consequences, is so largely divested of conscious or unconscious notions of the Christian faith that a far wider connotation than the verbal one which is ordinarily attached to the word "language" is needed. In the problem of communication as it poses itself today, language and translation comprises everything that translates in some manner the resolute commitment and solidarity of the Church with all the conditions, needs, and joys of men, wherever they may be, because the Lordship of Christ claims everything and everybody. (I refer also to what has been said in the third chapter on drama, symbolism, etc.) This explains why in many cases verbal silence combined with acts of disinterested, devoted identification and service may be the appropriate form of communication. It may be, for example, that the study project of the World Council of Churches in regard to the areas of rapid social change will appear in the long run to be an act of creative communication, though it is not at all intended as such. I hold the same conviction in regard to some of the pastoral letters of the Church in Holland. This wider conception of means of communication and language explains also why this discussion purposely has not tried to offer a full phenomenology of communication in the usual sense of the word, but has only partly dwelt on it, and has tried to suggest the whole compass of communication of the Christian message in the present time.

Fifthly, a point that requires particular attention in this matter of translation is the treasure of cardinal Biblical and theological concepts and expressions. Perhaps it is helpful to call them by a word come into vogue by Jung's psychology — "archetypal." Should we try to exchange this treasure for new terms, adapted to the thought patterns of

the modern world? Here my answer would be in the negative, in spite of the suspicion that I, by this negative answer, drop suddenly the line of flexibility, and become at
the decisive moment conservative. I gladly bear this suspicion because my real intention is different. Of course,
Biblical as well as classical theological language does not
escape the relativity and inadequacy belonging to all human speaking about the ultimately inexpressible. Biblical
and theological language is mythical (not mythological)
speaking on the revelation of God in definite *historical*
facts and persons, about *historical* facts of salvation. In this
combination of mythical speaking on *historical* (or pre-
and post-historical) facts of salvation lies the paradoxical
crux of Biblical revelation. (Mythical, one could say in
many respects also symbolical, speaking means speaking
in language that points to realities, spiritually or historically factual, which reveal and express the hidden and
true meaning in it. The cross of Christ, for instance, is a
fact. The affirmation that the reconciliation of God and
man, in Christ's sacrifice, is through the cleansing power
of his blood [self-surrender] is mythical speaking about
the cross.) Therefore, a constantly recurring critical consideration is wholesome, and can only yield good results
for an illuminating interpretation, provided the Lordship
of Christ and the living communion with him is an authentic reality.

The reason for the special place of this treasure of Biblical and theological language is not, in the first place, that
in it are preserved the continuity with the Church, its creative kerygma at the beginning, and the summits of decisive
interpretation in its history. This is an important point,
but still a secondary one. Above all, in regard to the Biblical thesaurus, the primary reason is that the cardinal Bibli-

cal concepts and expression about God, man, and the
world, in their cohesive unity, are unique in this sense
that they are discontinuous with all other expressions and
attitudes. I make bold to say that to say so is not a theological prejudice. My only theological prejudice is that I
answer to it with faith. It is, however, possible to demonstrate this proposition phenomenologically, without giving
the answer of faith. It can even occur, and in fact does
occur, that a phenomenologist, although without faith in
it, has a sharper eye for the particular structure of Biblical
revelation than a believing theologian, who is too much
determined by his narrowing and distorting outlook.

This primary reason does not apply in the same sense to
the theological thesaurus, because theology is interpretation
of the kerygma in terms of reasoning cogitation, and always
falls short of doing justice to the fullness, cohesion, and
dynamism of Biblical revelation. (This is the strong and
the weak point, the glory and the demonic danger, of theology.) All theologies together of the great Christian thinkers of all ages are only partial interpretations. The Bible
in its essential content proves itself, if one takes the trouble
to take it fully seriously. It needs no dogma of inspiration
to justify the claim for its authority, and to demonstrate
its transcendency above all theological systems and formu-
lations.

These remarks are made in order to make the point that
translation is certainly also necessary in regard to the Biblical thesaurus, but that the Church, daring as it may and
should be in this respect, must know that this thesaurus
is the Church's impregnable rock, and that only a new discovery and understanding of it will show that the cardinal
questions of man and life, in every generation and condition of culture, are laid bare in it. Translation has inces-

santly to go on in concrete life. It can and will be found, if one sees that the elementary Biblical words such as " sin," " redemption," etc., are not dogmatical propositions to be hurled indiscriminately at the heads of uninterested Christians and unbelievers, but symbols of fundamental life situations of every man in every time.

Let us come to some other, extremely vital, points in the whole strategy of communication of the Christian message, not only as a gospel, but as a vision of life and the world, which must be incarnated in lives and life patterns, and acquire audible voices.

Since the Amsterdam Assembly of the World Council of Churches in 1948, the question, What is the significance and place of the laity of the Church, in the Church and in the world? has increasingly acquired attention. Evanston published an important statement about it, which, without formulating it lengthily, contains a creative program of new insights and initiatives. The various lay movements in many countries and Churches, often of very different character, dependent or independent of the ecumenical movement, the world-wide discussion about the laity in professional life (cf. the second chapter on the Primitive Church), the concern about the lay issue, have all fired the imagination. This is not the place to enter into this whole matter. What concerns us in regard to the problem of communication is that here, in the tackling of the lay issue, we have the most vital possibility of an entirely new encounter of the Christian message in the world and with the world. Since the fourth century the significance of the laity for the life of the Church and for its spiritual strategy in the world has never been taken so seriously as today. We are still in the beginning, but the potentialities, especially for overcoming the breakdown of communication and for quite a new functioning of the Church in a secularized world, are not easily overestimated. It is literally a new adventure, with all its dangers and pitfalls, but out of sheer obedience to the Biblical conception of the Church it must be undertaken, working it out with fear and trembling, pressing " toward the mark for the prize of the high calling of God in Christ Jesus " (Phil. 3:14) .

One of the aspects is the necessity to seek for a new Christian style of life. In the so-called " Christian " world we have either no style or antiquated styles. The secular world is fundamentally styleless. This demand for a new Christian style of life is intrinsic to the whole question of finding an answer to the breakdown of communication and an expression of the vision of life, which the Christian faith, if well understood, implies. When carefully analyzed, the Christian " style of life " fundamentally means a new synthesis of Christian *liberty* and *asceticism,* from the point of view of training for the sake of the Kingdom of God. (An excellent book on the lay problem, communication, and a new style of life is Jacques Ellul's *Présence au monde moderne,* translated into English under the title *The Presence of the Kingdom.* Ellul is one of the most stimulating Christian thinkers and workers of today.)

In the first chapter of this book, I began by saying that communication is the fundamental fact of human existence. What has been said about communication also applies to the encounter with the non-Christian religions, the human encounter as well as the encounter on the level of intelligent discourse. In the second chapter we had occasion to say something about this encounter, but in the last two chapters we have taken into account only the " modern " situation of the West in order not to encompass too much. " *Qui trop embrasse, mal étreint* " (" Who tries to encompass too much, accomplishes little "). In Biblical perspective the communication of the Christian message, well understood, intends to show the way to restoring and establishing the right functioning of this fundamental fact, the communication *between* men. Being the fundamental fact of human existence, it is constantly endangered. Man knows that from bitter experience. The Christian should know it, with contrition and humility, when he sees how difficult it is in the ecumenical movement to develop not high ecclesiastical policy, but communication. The august prayer of our Lord, preserved to us in John 17:21, forcefully calls to mind the inner unity between communication *between* men and communication *of* the Christian message. So let us close our reflections by quoting it: " That they all may be one; as thou, Father, art in me, and I in thee [communication between], that they also may be one in us: that the world may believe that thou has sent me [communication of]."